ENDORSEM...

"*Campus Core* provides college students and campus ministers alike with a step-by-step guidebook to balancing the call of discipleship, glorifying God through academics, and preparing for life after college. I wish I had this information as a college student, and I'm grateful that Douglas Jacoby has taken the time to pass on this wisdom, so that we don't have to learn the hard way."

— Brian Campbell,
Campus Minister, Denver Church of Christ

"As a recent campus minister and as a parent of college students, I am grateful that Douglas has produced a comprehensive resource for campus ministry. In the Hampton Roads church we strive to provide direction in both the spiritual and academic concerns of our students, and *Campus Core* shores up these efforts to help students to thrive in Christ."

— Ed Anton,
Senior Minister, Hampton Roads Church

"At the heart of *Campus Core* is a narrative about evangelistic fearlessness. Learning from Douglas' stories is a refreshing way for Christians to acquire emotional intelligence and social awareness as they learn to share their faith. His stories of success are so impressive that it's humbling to me as a minister—yet he presents these without boasting. His matter-of-factness is one way of presenting this level of faithfulness as normative."

— Chris Zillman,
Campus Minister, Chicago Church of Christ

DR. DOUGLAS JACOBY

CAMPUS CORE

HOW TO HAVE AN IMPACT ON YOUR CAMPUS, GET GOOD GRADES, AND FIGURE OUT YOUR FUTURE

ILLUMINATION PUBLISHERS

CAMPUS CORE
© 2016 by Douglas Jacoby

About the author

Since 2003, Dr. Douglas Jacoby has been a freelance teacher and consultant. With degrees from Duke, Harvard, and Drew, he has written 30 books, recorded over 500 podcasts, and spoken in numerous cities in 115 nations around the world. Douglas is also pro- fessor of theology at Lincoln Christian University. For more information about the work, speaking schedule, and teaching ministry of Dr. Douglas Jacoby, see his website at www.DouglasJacoby.com.

Illumination Publishers
6010 Pinecreek Ridge Court, Spring, Texas 77379-2513
www.ipibooks.com

ILLUMINATION **IP**
PUBLISHERS

CONTENTS

LIMITATIONS OF THE BOOK 8

HOW TO USE THIS BOOK 9

I. OPPORTUNITY

1. Confidence:Walking Tall on Campus 12
2. Campus Evangelism: Preparation 17
3. Campus Evangelism: Sensitivity 31

II. ACADEMICS

4. How Intelligent Is My Study Strategy? 44
5. Perusing Huge Amounts of Material 55
6. Preparing Interesting Papers 59
7. Excelling in Examinations 62

III. ENGAGEMENT

8. Social Sciences 69
9. Humanities & the Arts 85
10. Mathematics & Physical Sciences 101
11. Professional Studies 114

IV. FOLLOW-THROUGH

12. Crucial Counsel for Campus Leaders:
    Healthy Campus Ministry 126
13. Full-Time Christian Work: God's Will for Me? 137
14. The Next Step: Grad School? 140
15. After College: Students for Life 144

V. APPENDIXES

Appendix A: Paying for My Education 151
Appendix B: Holistic Campus Ministry 159
Appendix C: Must-Have Books for Christian Students 166

Books by Douglas Jacoby

IPI books by Douglas Jacoby:

Advanced Christian Training
The Bible Quiz Book
Chariots of Fire
Genesis, Science & History
The God Who Dared
I Was Hungry!
Jesus and Islam
Life to the Full
The Lion Has Roared
The Powerful Delusion
Q&A I
Q&A II
*Christian Parenting in a
  Non-Christian World*
Shining Like Stars
The Spirit
Thrive!
True & Reasonable
What Happens After We Die?

Other Douglas Jacoby titles:

Answering Skeptics
Compelling Evidence
Equipping the Members
A Quick Overview of the Bible
What's the Truth About Heaven and Hell?
The Ultimate Bible Quiz Book
Your Bible Questions Answered

With translation into:

Chinese
Indonesian
Portuguese
Spanish
Russian
Vietnamese

Acknowledgements

Special thanks to Amy Morgan, Ed Anton, Daniel Berk, Brian Campbell, Kate Carman, Crystal Chan, John Durkota, Cameron Gifford, Phillip Goodchild, John Hanes, Amy Kho, Jan Kingan, Samuel Laing, Jim McCartney, Patrick Morrison, Barbara Porter, Joe Sciortino, Michael Shapiro, Joakim Siln, Katie Wenta, Jordanne Whitcomb, and Chris Zillman for looking at the manuscript and offering great advice.

Thanks also to all the campus ministers who found time to read the manuscript and point out where it needed more content or balance. I know you are working hard in the ministry of the word, and I trust your suggestions will continue to come in even after this first printing.

As always, I owe my publisher, Toney Mulhollan, the engine of IPI. This is our nineteenth book together. I do not know a harder-working man in the publishing field. Thanks for the last thirty years, Toney!

Limitations of the Book

We live in a time of swift technological and educational transition. Even in my own academic life, the third degree (1990s) was anything but traditional. It was a hybrid of residential and distance learning. The Internet was becoming increasingly important—and is now so fundamental that it may be difficult to imagine how it was back in the analog age. I teach *all* of my master's degree students online. The learning curve is steep—and things can be expected to continue to change: inverted classrooms, digital libraries, and so forth.

The majority of the principles highlighted in this book are applicable whether one attends a standard campus-based institution (dormitories, dining halls, lecturers with on-site offices, bachelor degree programs and higher, etc.) or is *studying* or leading ministries at predominantly commuter schools. However, in *the latter case* some of the material will not apply to you (parts of chapters 1, 2, 3, and 12). This is not intended to marginalize anyone; it's simply a limitation of a book of this size.

Last, 90% of my experience in campus ministry has come from working with university students in Europe and the United States. While I have visited scores of colleges on other continents, my work was never building the ministry—just supporting the ministry as a guest speaker. Although I hope that the principles written here will be applicable around the globe, I am quite sure that I have many cultural biases and blind spots. Thanks for bearing with me.

How to Use This Book

Hopefully we agree that it's a privilege to be a university student. In many nations this is only for the children of the elite. In other countries, women or certain minorities are blocked from higher education. If you are a student, your degree(s) will connect you with others, open doors, and confer greater earning power. Given that a college education is so valuable, and highly valued, dare we wander through the college years aimlessly? Never!

How can we be ambassadors for Christ on campus, bringing glory to God through everything we do? College is a time to learn (Luke 2:52), but it's also an ideal environment in which to become more like Christ (Col 1:28; Rom 8:29), engage in dialogue with fellow thinkers and explore new ideas (2 Cor 10:3–5), reach others with the gospel (2 Cor 2:14; 5:20), and think strategically about the next step (after graduation). Most of all, we want to thrive and mature as persons (John 10:10; 2 Pet 1:3–9). It is my hope that this book will aid in achieving all these core objectives.

Those serving in campus ministry are carrying on a vital and demanding work. Although this book is hardly a comprehensive manual, hopefully a number of the ideas within will prove useful in your ministry.

CORE AREA 1	Evangelism/Impact on Campus
CORE AREA 2	Academics/Getting the Grades
CORE AREA 3	Engagement/Using Your Mind
CORE AREA 4	Follow-Through/Your Next Life Stage

Reading Suggestions:
Section I – read straight through chapters 1–3
Section II – read straight through chapters 4–7
Section III – find the sections that match your classes in chapters 8–11
Section IV – read chapter 15, plus whatever else is relevant
Appendixes – As needed

I. OPPORTUNITY

As a student and a professor, I've spent many years on both sides, and have much to share, first and foremost about the mission. At the same time it may be obvious that the bulk of my experience was learned before many of my readers were even born. In the last two decades, I've remained strongly connected to campus ministry, yet more often as an adviser or invited speaker than as a worker in the trenches. I trust you won't hold this against me.

In this first section, "Opportunity," we'll learn why we should walk tall on campus, how we can maximize our evangelistic effectiveness as individuals and as a dynamic campus ministry, and how to share the message with the wisdom and gentleness that open doors for effective work.

CORE AREA 1
EVANGELISM/IMPACT ON CAMPUS

CORE AREA 2
ACADEMICS/GETTING THE GRADES

CORE AREA 3
ENGAGEMENT/USING YOUR MIND

CORE AREA 4
FOLLOW-THROUGH/YOUR NEXT LIFE STAGE

---

1. CONFIDENCE:
Walking Tall on Campus

I realize that not everyone loved school—but I did. Maybe that's because I came from a family that stressed education, and was fortunate to attend good schools. There were so many things to learn; education was an *adventure*. I think that college can be an exciting time for all of us, stimulating us to grow and flourish, bringing out the best in us. Yet it's not all about the degree. Campus is also an open *mission field* where we may share our faith with large numbers of people used to exposure to new ideas. They aren't hardened in their opinions, like many of the older generation (Eccl 12:1).

Those who became Christians in the university years, like my wife and me, and some of you reading this book, understand the tremendous potential of campus ministry.

Christian students should walk tall, confident as ambassadors for our Lord on campus. Of course there are lots of reasons we should walk tall. How about the fact that we are forgiven children of the King, or that the Spirit of Christ lives in us? But I'd like to offer another reason, one perhaps you haven't considered. To demonstrate, allow me to rewind—to my second semester of college.

Douglas the Door-Knocker Meets Dean of Students
When I was baptized in 1977 in my freshman year at Duke University, I immediately felt the desire to be evangelistic. While my hair and clothes were still wet from my baptism, I started knocking on the doors in my dorm, and my appearance proved to be a conversation starter. "Why are you dripping wet?" they asked. "I just got baptized," I joyfully explained. I then asked, "Have *you* been baptized?"

Door-knocking zeal led to some very interesting encounters. While many visitors came with me to our group Bible study, others declined the invitation, a few of them undoubtedly feeling badgered due to my repeated invitations. (What can I say? They *were* badgered—more on that in chapter 3.) Weekly invitations to fellow students soon led to an *invitation to me* to meet with my R.A. Surprisingly, when I got to his room, there were nearly twenty guys sitting around the room. None were too happy with my evangelistic methods—especially those who claimed to be Christians yet seldom shared their own faith. Let's just say this meeting didn't go all that well (although I felt like a true martyr). But it did lead to an invitation to another meeting. For this one, I, unlike some in my all-male dorm who had declined my invitations, didn't need to be invited twice. I was summoned by the Dean of Students.

The venue was the architecturally stunning Duke Chapel, centerpiece of West Campus and a great place to go and pray. My campus minister, whom I'd asked to accompany me, and I went upstairs to the office of the minister to the university. When we entered the room I was glad I'd brought a friend, since we were definitely outnumbered. The Dean of Students was present, among other dignitaries. Their message was simple: "Stop pressuring people. You're talking way too much about Christ, and people are complaining."

How does a young man with all the wisdom of nineteen years respond before so august an assembly? There was some collegial give and take, and they did make at least one reasonable point—that I needed to learn to respect people's decisions. Yet I let them know that my faith compelled me to continue to share the gospel. And then I took a page right out of their own playbook.

Beer, or Christ?
University funds were used to supply students in all dorms with copious quantities of beer.[1] Late at night, you really had to watch your step, or you might slip and fall on the linoleum floors, slick with hops and malt. Many campus groups exerted tremendous pressure to get students to party. Beer was free. Pot smoking was condoned nearly everywhere. One of my professors even encouraged us to find a boyfriend or girlfriend and have sex three times a week, in order to best appreciate our university experience. I made an offer. I would back off, I promised hypothetically, once the university did *their* part to reverse the pressure to live a godless life.

Of course I knew they weren't about to forbid beer. Before the stale-mated meeting came to a close, I drew their attention to the heritage of the university itself. A little-read plaque stood at the West Campus bus stop: "The aims of Duke University are to assert a faith in the eternal union of knowledge and religion set forth in the teachings and char-acter of Jesus Christ, the Son of God..."[2] I told them I agreed with this statement, and would happily abide by it. How was the university doing with that? Naturally, there was nothing they could say. On the one hand, these men claimed to be Christians themselves, yet they couldn't agree to abide by the plaque, since academia had changed so much in the last couple of centuries. Perhaps the real reason was that these men were no longer willing to make an exclusive commitment to Christ.

We were at an impasse. The dean was quiet. The minister to the uni-versity was abashed. The student representatives were not too pleased. My campus minister was beaming. Although a few minutes earlier they'd hinted at expulsion, I believed I just might be able to hang on till graduation.

Foundations
Interestingly, a peek into the history of many universities in North America or Europe reveals a significant drift from the founders' ide-als, as these were often connected with Christ. Educators often desired to bring glory to God. Today, in university circles, being an avid Bible reader is no longer taken as a mark of intelligence or good breeding. Obviously something happened. Education has been secularized.[3]

This becomes especially visible when one takes a look at official uni-versity mottos. Not all are religious, but a good number are. Perhaps the most revealing of academia's move away from faith is Harvard's motto: *Veritas*, Truth. But that isn't quite right. It was only after I graduated that I learned that the original motto had been shortened. It used to be *Veritas Christo et Ecclesiae*, Truth for Christ and Church. Not just truth as any modern or postmodern person might define it, but truth ordained by Christ for service through the church! In time the powers that be grew uncomfortable with *Veritas Christo et Eccle-siae*. They got rid of Christ and his church in one cut. But what does that leave? Truth without a context—truth no longer a solid rock on which we stand, but an orphan in a world without the Father. When we divorce truth from the Author of truth, we end up no more understanding truth than Pilate did before Jesus (John 18:38).[4]

Christians know that Christ is the *Logos*—the word, principle, reason—and in him all things fit together and make sense (John 1:1; Col 1:17). When we try to separate truth from God and godliness, we lose our way, our soul, and our inspiration. John Bowen, whose writing on this topic inspired me to look deeper into university mottos, comments on the difficulty of replacing Christian mottos with secular ones: "How do you express the rationale of the institution in a single phrase when there is no unifying principle, no sense that all knowledge is part of some greater whole? A motto such as 'Try harder' really doesn't cut it."[5] The unifying principle is Christ.

Service

Today's generation might believe that truth is nothing more than information—data, to be interpreted as we like. When we take into account the historic purposes and ideals of universities, we see that it was never about abstract "truth" or memorizing facts. Truth was meant to lead to service—not a six-digit salary, much less a four-year party-fueled rite of passage. We were to study for the Lord.

Confidence

Confidence comes from knowing we are in God's hands, that he is our loving Father. A consistent regimen of daily time in the Word and prayer amplifies this confidence and inspires others who are seeking God. Confidence also flows from preparation—when we are up to speed and on top of our coursework. In this chapter I've suggested a third basis for confidence: a remembrance of times when no one thought it odd that firm faith and the best of scholarship went together.

Christians may be made to feel, with their "outdated" morals and "intolerant" stand for truth, that they are out of step with the meaning of university education. Yet there's no need for embarrassment or apology. In a sense, it's the *unbelievers* who are marching out of step. More important, as Christians we can walk by the Spirit. May this perspective help you walk tall on campus.

---

[1] At the time, the drinking age was eighteen. Clubs received university funding, and kegs of beer were commonly purchased. The drinking age today is twenty-one, and dorm life has changed significantly as a result.

[2] The complete text reads: "The aims of Duke University are to assert a faith in the eternal union of knowledge and religion set forth in the teachings and character of Jesus Christ, the Son of God… to advance learning in all lines of truth; to defend scholarship against all false notions and ideals; to develop a Christian love of freedom and truth; to promote a sincere spirit of tolerance; to discourage all partisan and sectarian strife; and to render the largest permanent service to the individual, the state, the nation, and the church. Unto these ends shall the affairs of this University always be administered."

[3] Recommended: George Marsden, *The Outrageous Idea of Christian Scholarship.* There have been three great shifts in Western education, taking education from being more or less God-focused to being a means of serving self.

- **Shift 1:** From ministerial training to secular training. Most of the early colleges were founded to train clergy, like Harvard. Most of those early plaques have been forgotten. Even so, most colleges began with a biblical rationale for their program of education.

- **Shift 2:** From breadth of education to specialization. As a result, a broad liberal arts education nowadays is underappreciated. An "educated" person can now be ignorant in all areas of study apart from his own.

- **Shift 3:** From belief in truth to the rejection of (absolute) truth. When this happens, the pursuit of truth (once commonly agreed on) becomes the pursuit of self. "Truth" has now become plastic, a commodity or a tool.

[4] Besides Harvard, I attended four other universities. The motto of Duke was *Eruditio et Religio,* Learning and Religion. I did the tail end of my bachelors at Oxford University, where every day I saw the motto *Dominus Illuminatio Mea,* The Lord is my Light. When I pointed this out to my fellow students, they thought "How quaint." They had no idea that the motto comes from Psalm 27, much less that the original scholars of Oxford (founded 1096) would probably be taken aback by the godlessness of modern teaching. In London, the motto of Kings College is *Sancte et Sapienter,* With Holiness and Wisdom. Last, at Drew University it's *Doreán elábete, Doreán dote,* Freely you have received, freely give—a direct quote from Matthew 10 and a good reminder to any student who feels "entitled."

[5] John Bowen: *Journal of the American Scientific Affiliation* 66.4 (Dec 2014), 249. If you would like to hear my podcast on "University Mottos," it is accessible at http://www.douglasjacoby.com/universities-their-mottos/.

2. CAMPUS EVANGELISM:
Preparation

Students, God wants you to make an impact on campus. You're there as a representative of Christ, an ambassador (2 Cor 5:20). What an honor! The next two chapters specifically lay out an evangelistic strategy. In this chapter, we'll approach our subject from two angles, the personal and the corporate. The entire campus ministry needs a strategy, of course, yet we as individuals also need to think carefully about how we share the truth on campus.

PERSONAL PREPARATION

College usually means leaving the day-to-day care of the family system you grew up in, and it comes with forming new day-to-day routines, living arrangements, relationships, and responsibilities. Some students are prepared to do all of that and excel at coursework, too, while others are less well prepared. Recognizing the nature of our unpreparedness and the means for preparing might involve, among other tactics:

- Seeking wise counsel from students you admire for their faith
- Seeking advice from older persons
- Pacing yourself—possibly with provision for an extra semester or some summer work—so that no single academic term is a "killer"
- Enrolling with a fellow disciple and friend. (Sorry, applications aren't shared.)
- Taking a year off

Year Off?
It is wise to set yourself up for success. Are you a lot younger than your cohort of entering freshmen? Do you feel you need some time off? My wife took a year off between school and university. It was good for her, and such a gap year has helped other students, too. On the other hand, I went straight to college, even though I was on the young side, having turned eighteen just days before. Everyone is

different. Maybe you could serve overseas in the mission field for a year. Or, if finances are a major issue, you could work and save up to soften the blow of college tuition. For most of us, a year off may not be the way forward, but this strategy has helped many to return to school with more maturity and appreciation for the cost of living. It could be that a year off might save you from having an off year.

New Students
In most colleges, a Christian student swims in a sea of unbelief. There are far more unbelievers on campus than believers. 1 Peter frequently reminds us that we're called to suffer as exiles, foreigners, aliens, and strangers in the world (1 Pet 1:1, 17; 2:11, 21; 4:4; 5:9). You may no longer enjoy the support group you had in your high school youth ministry. Being outnumbered and misunderstood, it's imperative that we think things through. Peter pushes us to be prepared (1 Pet 3:15).

Gratitude
Maybe you're going to university for the first time. Unless you matriculated in the same city where your family lives, you are probably going to have to adjust to a new church family. Every church has strengths and weaknesses. If you make too many comparisons between the two congregations, it is easy to become critical and negative—whether about your previous situation or your new one. Strive to be thankful for the good, wherever you are.

Once again, collegiate education should be an honor. In my travels around the world I visit some countries where only 1 or 2% of the population attend college. It's not that they don't want it; it's prohibitively expensive, or open only to the wealthy. Be aware that your life, and certainly your education, is the envy of the world. (Just look around your campus at all of the people who are there from another country!) There's no room for ingratitude, complaining, or other forms of negativity. Actually, for evangelism gratitude is a strategy that goes a long way, since people are attracted to happy, grateful people.

Scheduling
Some students go to college and find that it's only as difficult as high school, or perhaps a bit easier. This may well be the case if your

school had high standards. This was the situation with me when I matriculated. You may end up with a lot of unscheduled time, so it would be a smart move to write out your schedule (classes, studying, student clubs, campus ministry, work, etc.), so that you keep pushing yourself to excel. If you're like most students, and find college is harder than high school, a smart schedule relentlessly respected will save you from failure and make the experience a joyful one. Students who plan well generally seem to have plenty of time for personal devotions, as well as time to share their faith with non-Christians. These students will experience significant personal growth in the college years.

Roommates

If you have a roommate, it's possible he or she will be a Christian, especially if you were already friends. Otherwise you'll be in the position of living with an outsider to the faith—someone who witnesses your life day in and day out. Your example can have a powerful impact on your roommate. Let's be kind and serving to our roommates.

Note: For some students, there is no "roommate." Campus housing may be unaffordable or unavailable. Of course there are some colleges that have no dorms—or dining halls—or (with virtual teaching) no classrooms. And some universities today don't even have campuses. This book is tailored to the conventional college situation.

Try to adapt the principles here and in the next section so that you can be your best for God and connect with other students.

You never know what the future holds; this man or woman may one day become a Christian because of your influence. I wish I'd been more respectful towards my roommates. One went on to become an eminent physician, another a historian, and a third a high school science teacher. One (my first) was killed when a locomotive struck and flattened his car late one night. And I have no idea what two others ended up doing. I wish we had shared more activities, talked more, and even prayed together. Roommates are precious, and we mustn't take them for granted. In a significant way, evangelism begins at home; for the college student, it begins in the dorm room.

Classmates

In your years on campus you will have the chance to speak to hundreds of persons in a natural setting. Be observant in the classroom. If you have a choice of seating, move around so that you can get to know your fellow students. Strike up conversations whenever you can, even when you're tired and feel selfish.

Workmates

These days many students must hold down part-time jobs in order to afford enormous tuition fees. This provides yet another pool of prospects in your evangelism. Don't live a double life: a Christian on campus, but an anonymous drone at the workplace. I recall one short-term job I held where I shared my faith on the floor, but never with the man who gave me a lift home every day. Naturally, I felt terribly guilty. Don't downplay or disguise your faith. Be the same person wherever you are—an ambassador for Christ.

Professors

Be respectful towards your professors. Even if it's a teaching assistant only a few years your senior, the Bible still tells us to be respectful towards all and to take advantage of our opportunities (1 Pet 2:17; Col 4:2–6). A bonus coming from cultivating such relationships is that they will come to know your character and may help defend you in the event of a conflict or provide you with a reference. As a result of students reaching out to teachers in an appropriate way, a large number of college professors have become disciples of Christ.

Open Eyes

The Lord may put dozens of people in our path, but we may not see them if we don't keep our eyes open! Eventually some of those Duke students I reached out to became Christians, but not during my freshman year. Actually, the first person I reached out to who was baptized into Christ was one of the janitors working in our dorm. Next, my brother and my mother became Christians, then a relative of a high school friend. Then, one of the January freshmen I'd help to reach out to was baptized—in the middle of the summer break. What a great first year!

Focus on fellow students. That's most natural and likely to be most effective. But keep your eyes open! Just because you're on campus doesn't mean you're limited to sharing on campus.

Returning Students

If you're returning to college, especially after a summer working, give careful thought to your evangelistic hopes. Last year you learned a lot of things—some the hard way. Wouldn't it be great if this year you were an even *better* witness of Christ?

I remember how on fire my heart for God was when I returned to Duke for my second year. I'd read the entire Bible. I'd shared Christ with high school friends and most of my family. Over the summer I'd had double quiet times most days, an hour on rising and a more generous time for study and prayer before going to bed. We were planning to have another Bible talk in my dorm room. In my first year I usually brought between two and five visitors to each group Bible discussion. Now I wanted to bring more. Are we easily satisfied, or do we press onward toward the goal (Php 3:12–14)? (I actually think I was doing better than I realized; staying the course would have been fine. It's not about the numbers, but about precious human beings with whom we can share the gospel and our lives as well [1 Thess 2:8].)

During the first week back I'd invited everyone I could. I knew that some of the upperclassmen would be more open after their summer break, and I certainly wasn't about to forget how receptive so many of the entering freshmen would be. Well before the Bible talk began, my room was full, the corridor just outside the door crammed with visitors. I later counted twenty-two people I had personally invited. What I hadn't reckoned with was that some of them would mention the meeting to friends. Twenty-nine visitors—this was crazy! With the other brothers and their guests, there was no way fifty could fit into a dorm room. We crossed the quad and poured into an empty classroom!

Feel like Elijah, Totally Outnumbered?

Before we move ahead, we should consider the possibility that you are studying at an institution without a campus ministry. That doesn't mean there can't be a thriving work there, even if you're the only one you know who is following Christ! When Elijah felt outnumbered in 1 Kings 18–19 (he was outnumbered, just not as badly as he thought[6]), he acted. And when fear and loneliness closed in on him, he withdrew, giving in to his emotions. With some divine encouragement, he got into gear again. There will be ups and downs for all of us. Just keep going.

As I was wrapping up my history degree at New College, Oxford, I felt quite alone. It was my first time out of North America, and I'd just spent several weeks traveling alone through Europe on a EuroRail Pass. I felt intimidated by Oxford, and it took a week for the anxiety to abate. ("You can do this, Douglas," I eventually told myself.) I missed the close fellowship of my campus ministry. The scholarship students seemed to be so "together," while I was socially awkward.

Some of them formed a Bible study group. Lots of us students came, but for me the diluted commitment and careless use of Scripture was deeply concerning. Should I start my own thing? Seven days went by, the idea surfacing in my thoughts repeatedly, as my conscience felt the burden more and more. Jeremiah 8:4 tells us, when you're down, don't lie there—get up! So I spread the word that there would be a Bible discussion group in my dorm room for anyone interested. Every week students came. I felt great, I found some good guys to study the Bible with, and I grew spiritually through what could have been a dry and uneventful time. More important, this set the stage (mentally and spiritually) for a future time when I'd be in a similar situation again.

That time came two years later, in 1982. As the only student in our ministry at the University of London (we'd planted the London Church of Christ in summer 1982), I knew God would bring the people if only I would just be faithful. (More on that in chapter 12.) The small step of faith at Oxford proved to be profoundly important, though I wasn't in a position to see this at the time. Sometimes we need to act in faith, even if we doubt our chances of success. Trust the Lord to do something with that mustard seed of faith!

Summary

In sum, here are a dozen pointers for rising freshmen and returning students alike:

- Determine whether you ought to consider taking a year off before entering university.
- If you have moved to your college from another city, don't make constant comparisons with your home church.
- Be grateful. Give thanks in all circumstances (1 Thess 5:18).
- Schedule wisely; don't leave things to chance. "Fortune favors the prepared." If you're smart, you'll have plenty of time to share Christ with your friends.
- Be respectful towards your roommate, the person who will see your faith day in and day out (1 Thess 4:12).
- Be on the lookout for classmates with whom you can strike up conversations.
- Perhaps you can sign up as a volunteer to guide prospective students (or groups of students) around the campus.
- If you have a job, don't forget people at your workplace.
- Don't talk yourself out of reaching out to your professors. They too need God (Eph 2:12).
- Keep your eyes open—many others may end up becoming Christians just *because* you're an evangelistic Christian (John 4:35).
- Returning students: resolve to have an even greater impact this year. There's always room for improvement. No one has mastered the art of evangelism; we're all somewhere on the learning curve.
- Even if you're the only disciple in your class or are part of a small ministry, think big and trust in the Lord (Prov 3:5–6).

If every campus disciple would be prepared, even in the absence of a "master plan" for the ministry as a whole, the Lord would act and probably amazing things would happen! This is not to say we should throw planning (and discretion) to the winds. Your campus ministry needs an overarching plan, too.

CAMPUS MINISTRY PREPARATION

The Goldmine

At the time I entered college, gold traded for about $300/oz. Three years later, when I began grad school, it was nearly $600 an ounce! Today it's over $1000—compared to $840/oz for platinum, $450/bitcoin, and $14/oz for silver—which makes me wish I'd bought gold! (At least my wedding band has tripled in value.) Similarly, campus ministry appreciates in value with every year; it's a wise investment.

Campus ministry is truly a goldmine. Tens of thousands have become Christians during their college years, and a great number of these go on to enter various fields of influence, including full-time Christian service. And yet, although the fruits of campus ministry have been so great, some churches in university cities don't prioritize campus ministry. (I say to myself, "This isn't good. What are they thinking?") Perhaps church leaders in college towns undervalue the treasure on which they're sitting because they're swamped with other responsibilities.

Bringing the gospel to university students makes excellent sense. If we're hoping for traction and leverage, this is the ministry to focus on:

- People often in their prime in terms of openness to the gospel,
- Who have many years before them, and
- Are well positioned to affect others for Christ in the university setting, who
- Will form a solid base in the local church, in terms of character and leadership, and
- Strengthen the church's financial base, as most graduates will have well-paying jobs.

In the Beginning

The beginning of the year is perhaps the most critical time in the life of a campus ministry.[7] If it is handled well, it can ensure lots of evangelistic personal Bible studies—and hence a good number of new Christians throughout the year. Otherwise, opportunities will be lost that perhaps will never be recovered. Since this is such a crucial time, you need to begin your work before the beginning of the academic term.

Before the Beginning

One good idea is to have a college leadership planning session before the year begins. Ideally, have a miniretreat; pull the group together and overnight somewhere. Establish such things as:

- Who will be in which group Bible study
- Where and when group Bible studies will meet
- What special activities should be planned for the coming year (retreats, play days, etc.)
- Making sure all the students are involved in good one-another relationships
- Having a time of Bible study, prayer and fellowship with a view to developing unity among campus leaders

Get into the dormitories around the campus at the earliest possible opportunity. Frequently, dorms and other facilities are open several days before the start of classes. Christian students might move in early, get themselves settled, and then begin helping others, building trust through serving. Harvard Law School was right next door to the Divinity School, where I lived. Helping the new students move in paid off, and resulted in the first conversions of the Law School ministry. These were elite students with great minds and lots of tough questions, but the Lord helped us not to be intimidated. *Everyone* needs to become a Christian, and anyone with the right heart *will* become a Christian.

Two Terrific Weeks

College ministries can limit themselves to slow growth by mishandling the first two weeks of the year. During those precious few days virtually everyone is looking for new friends. There is an openness to new relationships that may soon begin to fade. We should resist the urge to spend large quantities of time with one or two apparently receptive people. Meeting the masses is the need of the hour. Some students will benefit from setting personal goals for making new acquaintances. ("Today I'll reach out to five new people.")

It is difficult to keep track of all those new names and faces, so keep some kind of record. Lots of good evangelism time can be wasted by lack of good recordkeeping. In your first few minutes of conversation, mention the Bible discussion you attend. If people are receptive they'll pick up on it immediately. In this way you may get visitors coming without issuing a single invitation. Take special note of those who seem open and try to see them daily. The key in the first two weeks is not spending a lot of time with them, but making the time you do spend exciting. Keep the interactions short, sweet and consistent, and continue to meet new people each day.

During the first week don't take time to study personally with people; just get them to the Bible studies or Christian activities. In the second week, study only with the most responsive, and keep meeting new people. By making the most of these precious days you will surface the maximum number of open contacts.

Dorms

If the Garden of Eden was the paradise for mankind, then dormitories are the Christians' evangelistic paradise. They provide the best environment imaginable for seeking and saving the lost (Luke 19:10). Next to having a campus minister, having students in the dorms is a campus ministry's most obvious asset. Often students are encouraged to live off campus, to get out of the dorms. That may be good for some students, but overall I would make sure I had a very good reason to move off campus. (I lived eight of my eleven university years in the dorms; the immediate access to so many people in need of the gospel kept me on my toes.)

The apostle Paul was not afraid of leaders in his society, and neither should we be. The resident advisor, or R.A., is the most immediate symbol of authority most dorm residents face. It is important that Christians develop good relationships with the R.A. before the Bible studies begin. Then if anyone complains, you'll be seen as a friend and not as "that religious nut" in Room 104. Moreover, don't be intimidated by the R.A.s—countless times they have turned out not only to be "allies," but also have become Christians. Respect their authority, just as you strive to cultivate good relationships with other authorities in your life.

Most students on campus get to know few people outside of their dorms, classes, and clubs. In the university setting, you will typically encounter a number of small cliques, with only shallow interaction between groups. Our challenge is to get to know people in as many groups as possible, thereby expanding the number of people we can invite personally.

Clubs, student government, and sports are good ways of developing friendships, but be careful not to flood your schedule with activities that may be evangelistic "dead ends." Ideally, you want to find a number of varying activities on a casual basis, or maybe one that you truly love. One of the decisions I regretted was dropping out of intramural soccer. (This was my high school sport). When I became a Christian, I tended to view everything as black or white. Since soccer wasn't a "Christian" activity, it had to go. Yet I was meeting new people, staying in shape, and setting a more rounded example for others. What a shame to suddenly stop! The challenge is to become genuinely interested in things that interest other people, while never losing sight of the fact that the activities are tools, not ends in themselves.

Meals

Everyone likes to eat. Fortunately, in a university setting people are generally eating together with dozens, and often hundreds, of other people. Mealtimes are superb evangelistic opportunities. Regardless of how hectic the pace of life becomes, we must all take time to eat— which means that everyone has time to meet people. Even during exam times, when the campus ministry will need to trim back meetings, you can keep evangelism going by simply scheduling meals with other students. If you don't have someone to sit with, you can look for a group of people you have never met before and join them. The key is planning, and not just doing whatever comes most easily.

If you live off campus, it may still make sense to join the on-campus students in the dining halls, even though this may cost more than eating in your apartment. You might save valuable time, the food might even be better, and you'll definitely be in closer contact with non-Christians.

Classroom

Everyone has a favorite place to sit in a classroom. Many will sit in exactly the same seat for the entire term. As Christians we can deny ourselves that luxury; through the course of the semester we can move around the room, getting to know all the little groups in the classroom.

There is much to be said about your classroom example. Here are some suggestions about how to increase the brightness of your light:

- *Come early* – A person rushing in late to class is a nuisance to everyone. Better, if you're early you can chat with other students before class.

- *Do your homework* – Confused Christians make for timid ambassadors. Gain people's respect academically and they will listen to you about more important things. (Much more about this in Section II.)

- *Initiate with professors* – This will help you learn the material and feel more confident in class. It will also give you a chance to invite them to church. I carried out a survey among members of my fellowship who are university lecturers, many having become Christians through the example and words of their students. At the time, the global total was about 200 professors. Wow! They are people just like you and me.

- *Be joyful* – Demonstrate the peace that passes understanding—let people see your joy even in hard times, and they'll begin asking "Why?"

Risk-Taking

Sometimes I think we should take risks, without worrying about the outcome. My place at my first dorm at the University of London was for the summer only, after which I had to move out to let the undergraduates in. Right as I was moving, however, I noticed an advertisement for a new Bible study group. I knew enough people in the first dorm that it was natural for me to attend. After a couple of weeks of my being a part of this new group, the leader asked me privately if I would colead the group with him. He admitted he really didn't know the Bible very well, and I knew that the way he was going about things would only confirm the group members in their tepid faith. This was the opening I was hoping for. Imagine that—coleading a Bible study with someone who I didn't consider a biblical Christian!

Well, two months later we came to a parting of the ways. As soon as he realized that I didn't accept "once saved, always saved," I was no longer welcome. However, two of the men decided to come with me to the study I was coleading in my new dorm. Both of these pure-hearted men completed their veterinary degrees, later going on staff and serving as evangelists. I admit, the way we met may seem a little unorthodox to some, but if I hadn't been willing to take a risk—to infiltrate, if that's not too strong a word—a splendid opportunity would have been missed. Think outside the box!

Community/Commuter Colleges
In this situation, most students do not live in dorms (residence halls); some colleges do not even have housing available. That does not stop the work; it simply redirects it. The evangelistic focus shifts to the classes, cafeterias, and common rooms. Group Bible studies may need to take place at lunchtime, or in the evening, either in classrooms or in homes of Christians who live near the campus.

Recognition
Becoming a recognized student organization is especially helpful in all college ministries. Often all it takes is a list of signatures of persons studying at that institution. Check to see if your school has an office that oversees student organizations, and find out what their expectations are. Doing so brings both practical and spiritual benefits (Rom 13:1–7).

Conclusion
Campus ministry is a challenge and an opportunity like no other. It's a challenge because you're under constant scrutiny. There's no retreating—everyone sees your example. A consistent example makes an impact. Classmates will be drawn to those who can help others, who are giving, responsible, enthusiastic, and so on. Furthermore, religious classmates who aren't wholeheartedly following Christ, and feel somewhat guilty that *you* are sharing your faith while they aren't,

may be humbled and softened, and hopefully prepared to truly receive the gospel message.

It's also an incredible opportunity, for the same reasons. Never again will you have such easy access to so many people on a consistent basis. Not only that, but you're reaching out to people who may well be at the height of their receptivity to the gospel.

If you're a student, rejoice and enjoy it. If you're a church leader, find men and women to devote themselves to this fruitful harvest field. Invest in "gold" that will continue to grow in value.

---

[6] He felt like he was the only one worshiping Yahweh, and went into a deep funk. Yet he had forgotten the 100 true prophets who should have been his comrades. And when the Lord spoke, he learned that there were 7000 in Israel still holding on to a biblical faith. For more on this, see my little book *Chariots of Fire: Radical Life of the Prophet Elijah* (Spring, Texas: IPI, 2015).

[7] The next few pages have been adapted from my *Shining Like Stars* (1987, 2000, 2005), 45–50.

3. CAMPUS EVANGELISM:
Sensitivity

In the previous chapter we discussed the importance and logistics of preparation. These lessons have been honed over decades of outreach on countless campuses. Yet preparation can be emphasized to the detriment of sensitivity. ("We're ready for battle—now let's take our campus by storm!") What made Jesus so amazing, and so effective evangelistically, was his *personal* touch. Not only was he prepared, but also gentle, patient, and loving (Matt 11:28–30).

"Sensitivity" is a modern word; the Bible speaks of gentleness, a virtue undervalued in the "kick-down-the-door," "radical" evangelism sometimes promoted in conferences (though often, the message is really about consistency more than agressiveness). The Proverbs have several admonitions pertaining to sensitivity: 25:17, 20; 27:14.

1 Peter 3:15, "prepared to answer," is a favorite text of all ambassadors of Christ. Yet even here the criticism "a proof text out of context is a pretext" is valid. That is, when we yank a favorite passage out of context, we may be seeking an excuse to defend our tradition or interpretation. We tend to justify ourselves, and when we're in the rationalizing mode, any passage, or even a partial passage or phrase, will do.

Now, who will want to harm you if you are eager to do good? But even if you suffer for doing what is right, God will reward you for it. So don't worry or be afraid of their threats. Instead, you must worship Christ as Lord of your life. And if someone asks about your hope as a believer, always be ready to explain it. But do this in a gentle and respectful way. Keep your conscience clear. Then if people speak against you, they will be ashamed when they see what a good life you live because you belong to Christ (1 Peter 3:13–16, NLT).

Several things emerge from this wonderful text, addressed to a persecuted people by the aged apostle Peter (perhaps sixty or sixty-five at the time):

- We're surrounded by a society often antithetical to our ideals and contemptuous of Christianity. The Lord knows that this may cause us fear and anxiety, and he cares.

- Keeping Christ in our hearts, so that we are constantly aware of his presence, is the key both to overcoming fear and to evangelistic effectiveness.

- Preparation is important, since it allows us to give better explanations for the faith and also to remain unreactive. When anxiety spikes, things come out the wrong way. And forgetting that the Lord is with us gives anxiety free rein. That's why it's important to know our stuff—to be careful readers of the Word who take their stand on divine authority, not church tradition.

- Evangelism must be conducted with gentleness. The volume, tone, and content of our words can all exert pressure. Giving people time to process is also a good indicator of gentleness.

- We are to share with genuine respect. Even if the other person is in spiritual darkness, we are still to treat everyone with respect. Feigned humility will not work; we *really* need to honor and look for the good in others. Approach them as fellow travelers.

- Anytime we've damaged our conscience—been too harsh or engaged in any behavior at odds with the spirit of Christ—we lose moral authority, and the message may be obscured. If anyone is to be ashamed, let it not be Christ's ambassador, but those who reject the message.

- Often gentleness comes with age. I like to think that older means we're becoming softer, kinder—more like our Lord. There is some evidence that the apostles "mellowed" with age. (For example, compare John's original "name" in Mark 3:17 and his first epistle!) The right kind of aging and mellowing does *not* mean a loss of conviction. Rather, it means that conviction is channeled in different, more effective ways.

I don't want to run the risk that these principles remain abstract. Since I've made nearly every mistake an insensitive Bible-toter can make, sharing my faux pas will hopefully give these principles color. As you will see, I've begun to learn from my mistakes. Even though I continually commit new ones, I'm trying to follow Christ. For some people (like me) it isn't easy, but the Scriptures don't make gentleness and respect optional (Gal 5:22). After we consider personal sensitivity, we'll move on to address the sensitivity of the campus ministry as a whole.

SENSITIVITY ON THE PART OF INDIVIDUAL CHRISTIANS

It Doesn't Feel like Love

I remember one fellow I studied the Bible with. Mike was quite receptive, and we spent a lot of time together. He even invited me to his home, a couple of hours away, where his family warmly welcomed his new friend. Mike came to our spring retreat, where he was for the first time confronted with the possibility that he had been taught an inaccurate version of the gospel. Yet rather than giving him more time to process these new and somewhat disturbing ideas, I kept pushing, hounding him. One day he asked me, "What are you doing?" I said that I was reaching out to him. "Doug, honestly, I don't feel reached out to. Why do you care about me so much?" I replied that it was because I loved him. Mike's response: "Well, it doesn't feel like love."

What had happened? Once I believed Mike would become a Christian, instead of viewing him more and more like my soon-to-be brother, I saw him as a contact, another potential recruit. Nothing special about him. He could have been a different Duke student—that didn't matter. The whole point was to move him from A to B. Now don't misunderstand me. I'm not saying we shouldn't expect progress, or do what we can to help our friends to come to repentance. But I was becoming increasingly mechanical in my expectations and my behavior. In response, he drew back emotionally, which I interpreted as a signal that I needed to press harder. The cycle, of course, was unsustainable. We parted ways. Let's be sure that in our outreach we don't hound people.

The Almost Empty Bus

Sometimes we aren't tuned in to how others feel, or we miss basic social cues. Once at Duke I boarded the West Campus-East Campus bus when there was just one other student on board. I wanted to invite him to our Bible study. Feigning nonchalance, I meandered down the aisle and asked him if I might take the seat next to him. I really was trying to be casual and relatable, not to come on too strong. (I wonder what was going through that poor guy's mind. He was my prisoner for Christ, seated between the window and me. Obviously I wanted something.) When I invited him, his only escape would have been to climb over me! If I were going to do it over, I would have sat a row or two in front of him, said hello, and worked the conversation around to spiritual things. Sitting in front of him, not behind him, I could control the interaction (he couldn't turn his back on me). And I would be careful to be friendly, respectful, and gentle. What I actually did was to force myself on him—exactly the sort of behavior the Bible discourages.

Computer Cards in Your Face

One of my roommates decided to stop visiting our group discussion— but we still had two months before the end of the semester. I had been doing Bible studies with Scott on topics like sin, obedience, repentance, discipleship, and death to self. He wanted to believe in Christ, he said, but not the Christ I was presenting. Since he didn't want to keep studying the Bible with me, I decided to write a scripture on the back of a computer card and tape it on our door each morning. Every day Scott would see a new scripture. Eventually the entire door was covered. Thus did I present the Good News. (I doubt the person I was smothering felt there was anything "good" about it.)

Sharing the Scriptures is never a mechanical event, but I had not yet learned that lesson. Being by nature an introvert, being more comfortable writing than talking, and expecting others to respond logically to reasoning and verses the same way I would, I totally miscalculated. The next semester he asked for a different room, and so I ended up with a single room. It didn't dawn on me till years later than this was because no one else in our whole dorm (125 persons) was willing to move in with me!

I found my old roommate's address in a campus directory twenty years later. I wrote a letter of apology, which he said he appreciated.

Fifteen years after that, I realized he lived in the Atlanta area, not too far from us. Even better, one of the sisters in our congregation taught in the same school as he. I thought there might be an opening. I emailed Scott and asked if we might meet for coffee. I assured him that I wouldn't be pushy, that I had no agenda, and that I only wanted to make my apology in person. I hoped that after so many years he might be more receptive, or give me a second chance. He declined. A few more emails, and he made it clear that he never wanted to see me again. He wasn't mean, or emotional, but matter-of-fact. Sometimes our words and actions have long-term effects. If we are serious about representing Christ to others, we'd better be sure we're like Jesus, treating every person as an individual, with gentleness and respect. I failed to treat this roommate with either. Followers of Christ need to take this lesson seriously.

The Great Debate

In an undergraduate religion class I once went head to head with my professor. I asked a question early in class, he responded, but I didn't like the response. The discussion became a debate, and the debate filled the rest of our fifty minutes. No one else spoke except for the professor and me. Two days later the class met again. The debate continued! Hardly anyone else in class was able to get in a word edgewise. Word spread throughout the Religion Department. At the time I felt energized, empowered, proud for having taken a stand and pointing out the professor's errors to the class. The class had mixed feelings: some thanked me for my boldness; others were put off.

The disrespect I showed to an expert in world religions—this was his field, and he knew 100 times as much as I did—was monumental. Now when I engage in public debates, I attempt to demonstrate genuine respect, both by getting to know my opponent (reading his books, for example) and through patient interaction. There were plenty of times in my masters and doctoral classes that I thought differently than the professor. In time I learned to pick my battles carefully, and even to bring an element of playfulness to the disagreement. Learning to disagree with respect, humor, and give-and-take makes it a lot more likely that your words will register with those listening.

Fragile: Handle with Care

During my summer at Oxford, I focused on sharing the good news with three persons. I felt it was going well with two men, and there was also a woman who seemed receptive. One day, out of the blue—so it seemed—one of the program directors pulled me aside and cautioned me. "Watch your step, Doug. This girl is fragile. She's talking about 'conversion,' but she has some psychological issues. You need to *back off.*" And I did. Since everyone is different, and because the gospel message is potentially so hard-hitting, we need to exercise special care with those who are vulnerable. Most likely this woman was not ready to hear the message, but later she might have been. Somewhere down the road, another disciple would help her. It was not to be me.

One of Isaiah's prophecies said that the Messiah would not exert pressure so as to break a bruised reed, or snuff out a smoldering wick (Isa 42:3; Matt 12:20). I did not understand this concept as a young Christian, but many psychology and counseling classes—and a few decades—later, I am grieved to think how many people I have bruised. My last semester at Duke I had a Christian roommate. He wasn't as tough or confident as I, although he was a great guy. I now realize how much I intimidated him. I was way too forceful. I attended a Duke Reunion twenty years after we said good-bye. All of a sudden we were standing next to each other. In a flash, I saw him step back, as a dark shadow of fear moved across his face. A grown man, highly respected in his field, probably viewed as both competent and confident—but still jumpy around me. Do we realize that there are consequences to our words and deeds—and if our presentation of Christ is offensive, it may drive people away instead of drawing people to him.

We Can Change!

As a graduate student, I began to learn a good kind of caution. Classroom interactions were more respectful. At Harvard, I began initiating meals with professors. I still needed to be more respectful towards other students. At this time in my life, whenever anyone had a different interpretation than mine, I had a single thought: *One of us is wrong, and it isn't me.* Biblically speaking, there are quite a few matters over which we might disagree, without that meaning one of us is a "false prophet." Only if someone has distorted or rejected the gospel does anyone need to slap on them the "false prophet" label.

I made it through my two years at Harvard without any major scrapes. People were becoming Christians. I was still not very mature emotionally, but I was beginning to soften. Shortly before I moved to London to help plant a church, *and* to enroll in the MPhil program at Kings College, the Dean of Harvard Divinity School called me into his office. He cautioned me on how I shared my conservative Christian views in a liberal establishment. "Douglas, if you think *we're* liberal, just wait till you get to the University of London."[8] That comment prepared me to have better interactions with scholars with whom I was in fundamental disagreement. At Kings, I spent much time with students, chaplains, professors, and even journalists—and know that I showed much greater respect than I would have shown before those exciting years in Cambridge. I was now a five-year-old Christian.

Overall, my time at Kings went swimmingly. Often I was called to meetings with concerned parents. I also had numerous meetings with the wardens of the residence halls, doing all I could to build trust. The most intense meetings were typically initiated by other religious groups that disagreed with our strong emphasis on discipleship. They were miffed that our ministry was growing so quickly—especially when they were losing members. I never finished the degree at Kings, but I did learn a good many things I'm still using today, both academic and evangelistic.

Soon church work, fatherhood, and travel kept me busy. In 1996, fifteen years after the London planting, a friend convinced me to enroll in a doctorate of ministry degree program at Drew University. Things there went more smoothly, and as you may have predicted, I put that down to greater respect towards students and professors alike. The point is simple: we can change. We can grow into the likeness of Christ, though this takes faith and reliance on the Holy Spirit. I still have far to go (just ask anyone who knows me well), but this growing conviction has transformed how I relate to others publicly as well as privately. Interestingly, several brothers and sisters in Christ who have watched my debates have told me that I "won" the debates decisively because of my respect and humility, even more than by what I actually said.

SENSITIVITY ON THE PART OF THE CAMPUS MINISTRY

- What goes for us as individuals goes double for the campus ministry. What is the attitude of your campus ministry towards other groups?
- What sort of rapport does your group have with the university?
- Are your members aware of any rules governing proselytizing on campus?
- How do you interact with other religious groups on campus? Are you aware of their basic teachings? Of the areas where you agree and where you differ?
- Do you have a reputation on campus? What do people say about you?

Disrespect for Other Groups

From my earliest days as a young disciple, we had run-ins with other Christian groups. We felt it was very important to show that our group was right and theirs was wrong, and would make disparaging comments about them. I don't mean to say that they were taking a stand for the truth, because to this day I believe they had a deficit of courage and were unwilling to call their members to holy living. In the Bible, that's a big deal. "Make every effort to live in peace with everyone and to be holy; without holiness no one will see the Lord" (Heb 12:14; see also 2 Tim 2:23–25).

How can we show proper respect for other religious groups on campus? For one, keeping them in the loop on any special events you are hosting is a good idea. Invite them to come. On occasion, be willing to attend one of their events.

On several occasions I've been invited to lecture on Muslim university campuses. Muslims have ended up hearing the gospel and becoming followers of Christ. Yet without respect and communication there would never have been opportunities like these. If we treat Muslims,

Jews, and adherents of other world religions with respect, shouldn't we treat other "tribes" of Christians with at least the same degree of respect? Perhaps we feel threatened by them, unable to see the good—perhaps secretly hoping for them to fail?

I remember one time there was a double-booking. Minutes after our group showed up for a special meeting we had booked, so did another group, a "signs and wonders" ministry. I knew that the lesson I was giving might be hard for the other group to hear, but all the same I asked the leader and his group if they would like to join us. What began as an awkward moment quickly resolved itself, and it was obvious to all that we had no interest in being sectarians.

Work with (Not against) the University
There is seldom any reason for an adversarial relationship between your campus ministry and the university. Respect the guidelines. Consider yourself *part of* the campus community, instead of being at odds with the university. Of course, there are some values and programs that true Christians can never support—I am not nǎve about that. Yet most of us could do better collaborating with campus officials. Cultivate relationships with key persons in your college or university.

Working within the system instead of attacking it from without, your group may even be able to tap into the university budget. You can bring in a guest speaker—perhaps through the department of religion or philosophy—and the university will underwrite the event. Many times, through the smart thinking of friends, I've been invited in just this way. Once the University of Alaska flew me up and even provided simultaneous translation for the deaf for my series on the paranormal. One of my debates was completely funded out of the purse of the University of Florida. I've spoken a number of times in Ivy League schools, and they picked up the tab. One of the most rewarding events was an evening at Harvard on the Dead Sea Scrolls and reasons to trust the Scriptures. My presentation was in the same building where thirty years earlier I'd worked as a part-time janitor. Now I was back (without the vacuum cleaner) and everyone was calling me "sir." I got a kick out of that, and I think the audience did too, when I shared it with them.

The apostles won many followers for Christ as they worked within the "system" of Judaism. In Athens the apostle Paul worked the system (Acts 17:16–34). Because he knew how people thought and how things worked, he was able to receive an invitation to speak to an important assembly, the Areopagus. His presentation led to the planting of a Christian church in that great city. Being respectful and playing by the rules pays off:

- Linking arms with other groups means their connections and resources may become yours. From time to time common cause can be made, for example in campus or community service events. Or you might jointly invite an outside speaker.

- Tapping into funds already designated for outside speakers is smart. Usually all it takes is being an official group or club on campus.

- Prospective members for your ministry may be referred to you by others in the university, when you are known for respect towards others, quality presentations, and being team players.

- You may end up with someone well placed in the university system who will vouch for your character in the event your group is ever misrepresented—something sure to happen sooner or later (2 Tim 3:12; 1 Pet 2:12).

Love

"People don't care how much you know until they know how much you care" is an old saw, but a good one. Let's be prepared—know our stuff, have a plan, strategize. But let's also be like Jesus. We should interact individually and corporately with gentleness and respect—which are both part of love.[9] That's what will make a campus ministry really take off, bearing fruit that will last.

[8] Not that I found Kings to be more liberal than Harvard. Perhaps the Dean was thinking of the point that Harvard celebrated diversity. For example, along with conservative Christian groups, Muslims and Buddhists were welcomed, without any attempt to influence them for Christ. There was also a very large gay and lesbian club on campus.

[9] If you have been in campus ministry for some time and would appreciate a critique of traditional evangelistic techniques, watch the Paradigm Shift series and webinar, accessible at www.jacksonvillechurch.tv/next-steps/.

II. ACADEMICS

Whatever your hand finds to do, do it with all your might.

(Ecclesiastes 9:10)

God expects excellence of students; if not excellent results, at least a genuine effort. Effort is wholeheartedness, as in the scripture above. This should be a *core* value for any student. Yet too often Christians are zealous in other areas—perhaps commendably so—but not in the arena of academics. When some (undisciplined) students become Christians, they use evangelism or "church" as excuses for mediocrity. Studying isn't an unspiritual activity; it's a God-given responsibility. What's unspiritual is *neglect*. Unless they persevere, students suffer loss in character, discipline, confidence, and credibility—not to mention future prospects.

CORE AREA 1
EVANGELISM/IMPACT ON CAMPUS

CORE AREA 2
ACADEMICS/GETTING THE GRADES

CORE AREA 3
ENGAGEMENT/USING YOUR MIND

CORE AREA 4
FOLLOW-THROUGH/YOUR NEXT LIFE STAGE

In this book, special emphasis is given to evangelism and academics, as these activities are often in competition with one another instead of being complementary activities. The second section of the book is designed to help us to be *smarter* students. We'll examine a wide range of healthy study habits. After addressing general principles (chapter 4), we'll move on to the specific areas of reading, papers, and exams (chapters 5–7).

Think you're a smart student? Let's find out.

4. HOW INTELLIGENT IS MY STUDY STRATEGY?

The scholarship committee informed me that due to a low GPA, my scholarship had been revoked. At the time, the A.B. Duke Scholarship included not only a financial award (today it's a full ride), but also a term at Oxford University. This was not a happy day. But let me rewind the tape to four semesters earlier.

In high school I'd been a 4.0 student,[10] and even got to give the valedictory address. I assumed I could coast through my classes at Duke the same way I did in the private school I had been fortunate to attend. Yet two things happened in my first term. I became a Christian, and I got a C in Psychology (events not connected). This grade was determined solely by multiple choice tests. Let's just say that if I didn't agree with the experts, I would give the answer that I liked best—even if I knew it was wrong. That one poor grade, blended with my As in European History, Western Religions, and Vector Calculus, meant I was no longer cruising at the top of the student body. Rather, one third of the student body was above me!

I felt a combination of despair and apathy. "It'll be impossible to climb back up," I thought, "and besides, it's not that important anyway. If I can just keep a B average, then I will have loads of extra time for the things of the Lord, and the scholarship committee will be okay with me." Now I don't mean to say that a B is a bad grade; many students do their best and are pleased with Bs. Yet for me, this was a matter of character.

To continue the narrative, for the next few semesters I did the minimum, hovering at the B level. Soon it was finals time—springtime, when everybody would rather be outside, not stuck in a library or behind a typewriter (a 20th century writing device.) It was then that I discovered coffee and all-nighters—and the experience of sleeping only six hours in three days. I was so bleary-eyed that I only made it through half of my Latin American History test. (At the time, I really didn't like that class—ever had one of those?)

I scribbled a request on the exam booklet explaining that I was exhausted, and asked my professor whether he couldn't just grade me as though I'd finished *both* halves. In effect, I was requesting that he double my exam grade. (That was bold!) He refused—as well he should have—which left me with my F on the final exam, a D+ in the course and, more important, a cumulative GPA of 2.9. Oops.

Finally the nineteen-year-old version of my present self was sobered. At first I played it down: "Big deal. So I'll lose my scholarship. They're only paying $500 a semester anyway, and I didn't really want to go to Oxford anyhow." Fortunately some older and wiser friends talked sense into me. "What kind of example are you setting for those you want to win over, especially your family members? Don't just roll over and die—do something!"

I begged the committee if there was any way to win back the scholarship through summer courses, averaging the grades into my cumulative GPA. After they agreed, I clearly recall being determined to do my very best from now on. Although I had been a follower of Christ for nearly two years, I'd been using God and Bible study and church and evangelism as excuses for mediocrity. This for me was like a second repentance. I don't want any of you to go through what I did, so pay attention; the important stuff comes next.

PRINCIPLES

Principles are timeless; they apply to all people in all cultures in all generations. As Christians, we want to be men and women of principle. Practicals, on the other hand, vary with culture, societal norms, technology, etc. Practical advice that works well in the US might flop in Japan, even though the underlying principles are the same.

Key principles for students are excellence, discipline, integrity, flexibility, focus, and awareness of the Lord—for whose glory we are students in the first place. We will begin with some important principles for all of us, whether we live in the US or Canada, Singapore or

Indonesia, Nigeria or Colombia. We'll then offer twenty practicals—hopefully, most will be relevant to your situation.

Excellence

The first principle is that of excellence. We won't all reach the same level academically, but there's no reason we can't all make equal exertions to give the Lord our best.

> *Whatever you do, work at it with all your heart, as working for the Lord, not for human masters... It is the Lord Christ you are serving* (Colossians 3:23–24).

"Whatever" includes academics. Are we wholehearted? Who are we serving—our professors, ourselves, or the Lord Christ? And yet few campus ministries I've seen place any emphasis on academic excellence. (I know this because I've spoken on 200 campuses, and I ask probing questions.) Most ministries are more likely to hold their students accountable for showing up to meetings or for sharing with their classmates than for setting a good example in the classroom.

It's easy to see how failure in one area leads to failure in another. When we have a clear conscience about our studies, we're more confident; we're more likely to be available to help out another student who's struggling; and we have more credibility when we reach out to fellow students—not to mention our lecturers.

Recently my wife and I spoke at a student awards program in Manila. Extra honor was given to students who had distinguished themselves. This not only made them feel great, but also brought honor to their families (who attended the event). The Filipinos are right on track.

This reminded us of our campus ministry when we first moved to the United States (1992). In Philadelphia, with the support of our church elders, we set up a Student Honor Society. At the end of each semester, those who maintained an exemplary GPA (we made 3.3 the target) were singled out for congratulation. Those who kept up a high GPA (3.5 or higher) received a handshake from the elders, together with a $50 check.

Aiming for excellence is a *spiritual* issue. It is Christ we should be serving, and he is not happy with a sloppy, indifferent attitude towards education.

This year I'm studying the Proverbs intensively, and discovering so many gems, like this one:

> *Do you see a man skillful in his work?*
> *He will stand before kings;*
> *he will not stand before obscure men* (Prov 22:29 ESV).

Whether or not we apply ourselves has implications for our future prospects. "The cream rises to the top" is a popular proverb that describes biblical figures like Joseph and Daniel. Do you aim high? Is striving after excellence one of your traits?

Consciousness of God

A spirit of excellence is boosted by awareness of the Lord—the second principle. Biblical men and women of faith, like Daniel, Joseph, Esther, Ezra, Paul, Priscilla, and Aquila lived in the presence of God. They were truly aware that behind the thin veil separating the visible world from the invisible one, God himself was watching.

Peter makes a similar point in 1 Peter 3:13–15, where he tells us that even when we are persecuted, conscious awareness of Jesus Christ keeps us from being intimidated, just as the believing wife may live free from fear and even win over an unbelieving husband by focusing on the Lord (1 Peter 3:1–6). In every class we attend, our prayer should be that we discern God's will for us and truly live (and study) in his presence.

Discipline

Anything worthwhile in life is going to require focus, persistence, and discipline. Discipline makes us get up with the alarm, no matter how tired we feel. Discipline brings us to every class, arriving on time. With discipline, we'll probably never have to beg for an extension for our late assignment.

Now don't think that a disciplined person automatically gets good grades. Even when I was losing my scholarship, I was still a disciplined person. I wasn't goofing off, but my priorities were skewed. I was busy, but not always busy with the right things. I rationalized being in the academic doldrums by telling myself I was doing well spiritually—attending every possible church or campus ministry meeting possible, knocking on 50–100 doors a week in cold-contact evangelism, wearing out Bible after Bible. Unfortunately, the world is filled with highly intelligent and otherwise disciplined people who fail to apply themselves academically.

Integrity

The word "integrity" comes from the Latin word for whole (*integer*, like whole numbers). When we have integrity, we are "whole" in the sense that we're authentic and sincere, persons of character. Highly important for students is the quality of honesty. The problem isn't just the epidemic levels of cheating today, but educators' and students' anemic response to it. Even worse, cheating in the college years easily morphs into cheating in the marriage (destroying families for the temporary pleasures of sin), as well as cheating in the marketplace (overcharging, deceptive advertising, and unethical "favors for friends" come to mind). The pressures to deceive only increase the older we grow and the more complex our lives become.

At any rate, to pass off someone else's work as our own is academic theft. The Lord God hates dishonesty (Prov 6:16–17). Liars do not fare well in the Bible (1 Tim 1:10; Rev 21:8). Let's be resolved neither to cheat nor to connive with others who are cheating.

Holy Escapism?

One further caution: Christians love fellowship and derive a lot of their sense of worth from relationships with fellow believers, as well as from outreach to the lost. Yet when it's time to study, fellowship can be a form of escapism—with a holy rationalization.

Maybe your campus group has planned a games evening. You'd love to join, yet a big project is due in two days and your conscience is telling you to head to the library. Don't expect your campus leaders to force you to study. They may not understand your situation. You do, however. Seek advice and understand that there are times when "spiritual" activities—regular meetings or special events or even evangelism—may not be God's will for you.

I was such a restless young Christian. After studying for thirty minutes, I'd get up from my desk, go for a walk, and look for people to invite to my group Bible study. That made me feel great—all the adrenaline and endorphins! But it also guaranteed that I'd be no more than an average student. This dynamic was exactly what led to my losing the scholarship. I wasn't a lazy person, but I'd exchanged essential study time for "spiritual" activities that I found more rewarding. When two choices are both good (like fellowship and studying), we need wisdom to discern what is *best* (Php 1:10). Become aware of the ways we may (perhaps unwittingly) excuse ourselves from the path of excellence.

Focus and Flexibility
There are many things we can do to stay limber mentally so that we can bear down on our studies when we need to, whether it's time to complete a project, begin researching a paper, or excel during final exam time.

We all want to be effective as students. At the same time, nearly every student is willing to admit shortcomings in discipline. Unlike God, we don't have all knowledge. We cannot be in every place at the same time, nor can we manage without sleep (1 Cor 13:2; Ps 121:3–4). Perhaps you are looking forward to finding concrete solutions to help you improve your focus.

PRACTICALS

The practicals below have served me well as a student, and even in life after college. Through my years at five universities I had plenty of time to refine my approach. Here I share a few principles that could radically transform your own effectiveness in homework and study habits.

1. *Prioritize classes and assignments.* Think clearly. What's your easiest/hardest class? For which one should you allocate the most time? Given the due date, when do you need to begin work on the term paper?

2. *No all-nighters.* Waiting till the last possible moment, then missing a whole night's sleep as we abuse our poor bodies in order to turn in an assignment thirty seconds before it's due is no way to live. All-nighters are, rather, an admission of failure to plan wisely (Prov 22:3).

3. *Put your plan on paper.* Don't leave things to chance. When it's written out, it's easier to tell whether it makes sense. Some students approach their studies without any real strategy. You might get away with it in the third grade, but in our late teens and twenties we need to think like adults (1 Cor 14:20; Heb 5:14; James 1:4).

4. *Set goals* and, for the larger projects, subgoals.

5. *Frequently review your plan.* Lists, schedules, and strategies frequently need tweaking. Feel free to revise or jettison, as needed, though don't feel free to *ignore* your plan.

6. *Create personal incentives.* For example, I will award myself an ice cream if I study History three hours today, or finish that translation, or get out of the lab in under three hours.

7. *Beware "the fallacy of the sponge."* Imagine a sponge, immersed in water and heavy with liquid. You can squeeze most of the water out by pressing your hands together with some force. Double the force, and a little more drips out. Using 80% of your strength is efficient; after that, there are diminishing returns. It's simply not worth the extra work required to get *all* the water out! Don't study every hour until exam time. Allow time for rejuvenation of weary brain cells. You'll get a higher grade.

8. *Schedule free time as well.* It's easy to overcommit, taking too heavy a course load, being involved in unnecessary extracurricular activities, or setting unrealistic goals ("I'm going to study fifteen hours on Saturday."). I call my system "blocks and breaks" and still use this strategy as I balance day-to-day responsibilities (correspondence, writing, recording, appointments, studying, and

planning). I'll study from 2:00 to 2:50, then go for a walk, or get something to drink, until resuming work at 3:00. If it's been many hours at the grindstone, the break may be longer, perhaps thirty minutes or an hour. I alternate between periods of high functioning and "down time." A power nap works well for some students.

9. *A day off a week is a great principle.* My father told me he learned this when he was working full time while studying for the arduous actuarial exams. He'd prepare only until the day before the exam. Though 85% of his classmates failed out of the program, he made it. (Could it be that some of his classmates overdid it?) Sabbath wisdom benefits students. You'll be fresher, waste less time, and think more clearly.

10. *Concentrate.* Concentration begins not when we sit down to work, but when we get up in the morning, when we decide what to eat, and even when we retire the night before. Sluggishness can be prevented when we eat well, rest sufficiently, drink enough fluids, and stay active physically. Further tips:

    • The room where you study should be on the cool side, and not too stuffy.

    • Make sure you have enough space to spread out your materials. Ideally this should be your personal space (don't be a nuisance to others). Your bed is not the personal space I refer to!

    • Many of us work best in a quiet room. Is there music playing? That may be fine, though probably not if there are words. Are there others in the room? If they're distracted or distracting, go somewhere else. Take account of your ideal study environment.

    • Stray thoughts are bound to come, so keep some scratch paper handy for those important (but extraneous) ideas that may otherwise torpedo your efforts. Jot down a note and get back to it once your work is done.

    • In the classroom, you may want to sit relatively near the front. Make sure there's a clear view of the screen, or whatever part of the class is involved in the learning process. Make eye contact with the teacher.

    • Don't sit next to distracting persons (whispering, eating, passing notes…). Note who the sharper students are.

11. *Interact with teachers.* Don't keep professors at a distance. Answer questions, ask questions, solicit suggestions. Be a servant in the classroom (though not obsequiously).

12. *Be punctual.* Don't push it. Arrive to class on time, submit assignments on time, and stay on course.

13. *Seek input* in the area of academics. Get input, as needed, from professors, lecturers, and fellow classmates.

14. *Attend every class.* This is important for your example, even if you already know the material. If you miss a class, get the notes from a student you trust—not just from anybody who happened to be in the room.

15. *Take careful notes.* If they're sloppy, you won't derive much benefit when it's time to review them. If you're writing in books or textbooks, review your notations once you finish the book. Keep the most useful books; sell the others at the end of the term.

16. *Catch up on any missed lectures.* Once in a while you may have to miss a class (sickness, funeral, schedule conflict). Do what you can to catch up.

17. *Strike while the iron is hot.* Review your notes within 24 to 48 hours; after this time, you're beginning to lose the learning advantage. Go through homework assignments within a day of receiving them, and plan how you will get them done.

18. *Beware false comparisons.* Even with excellent preparation, you may not get the highest test mark in the class. You're you, not someone else, and we all have different abilities. Be content with who you are. Just do your best. Compare yourself to others with respect to attitude and discipline, not just results (grades).

19. *Don't be a perfectionist.* The goal is to live in the presence of God and serve the Lord Christ. Maturity is more important than perfection. Don't forget to take into account that "time and chance happen to [us] all" (Eccl 9:11). Accept network crashes, miscommunications, illness or death, human error, and so on, without having a personal meltdown.

20. *Don't whine.* "I don't have time" is the excuse of the weakling, the coward, and the loser. You have time to do all the Lord would have you do. Take ownership of your schedule.

Back on Track

Maybe you, like me, were—or are—off track. Hopefully the suggestions in these chapters will really make a difference in your situation. We left off our story with me about to forfeit the scholarship. Let me tell you how it turned out. That summer I took two intensive classes, receiving an A and an A+. The committee counted them in the GPA for my first two years—now pulling it up a whisker over 3.0. The scholarship was saved! And I spent a term at Oxford—my first time outside North America, in a country where I would eventually move on a mission team, become an evangelist, and find a wife. I'm so glad I listened to advice and didn't let the scholarship go!

In my third (final) year at Duke, my GPA was around 3.6, though the cumulative GPA was lower—dragged down by my first four semesters. I graduated *cum laude,* but that modest distinction only reminded me of my sophomoric foolishness. Yet I *had* learned my lesson. For me the point wasn't so much to study harder as to stop using my faith as an excuse for indiscipline.

Next, at Harvard, I was determined to go all out. As I finished up my masters, I was at the 3.8 level. And years later, doing my doctorate at Drew, I was consistently hitting 4.25—the highest GPA possible at that institution. My professors actually told me to slow down! I guess I still hadn't found the right balance, but there's no question I was back on track. I would never again use the Lord as a pretext for intellectual laziness.

Let's take academics seriously, neither "coasting" nor going over the top. Living a well-rounded and balanced life enhances the gospel and infuses others with hope and faith. Students who live out their faith succeed both academically and spiritually.[11]

These are principles to live by. If you're a student, they will enable you to enjoy your student years and look back on them without regret.

---

[10] If you're not familiar with the standard American (US) grading system, this will help. A = 4.0, B = 3.0, C = 2.0, D = 1.0. The lowest grade possible is a D; the highest used to be A, although in some institutions it's an A+ (4.3). Minus grades subtract 0.3 points. Thus A- = 3.7 and C- = 1.7. Plus grades add 0.3. Thus B+ = 3.3. Theoretically the average grade should be B-/C+, or 2.5, though not a few professors dish out As and Bs for clearly substandard work. GPA is grade point average, the average of your class marks. Here's how it works. If this semester you receive one B-, three Bs, and an A, your GPA = [2.7 + 3 x 3.0 + 4.0] / 5 = 3.14.

[11] According to a Family Research Council study, the GPAs of students involved in religious activities are 14% higher than those not involved (OneNewsNow 9/14/10).

5. PERUSING HUGE AMOUNTS OF MATERIAL

During undergrad days I learned something about reading strategy, especially in a political science course with heavy weekly reading assignments. This came in useful in grad school, too, especially when I was doing a doctorate as a full-time church leader, international traveler, and father of three. I found myself in a position that required me to maximize reading while time was at a premium.

Most books don't require you to read every word to understand the material, and various strategies can simplify your task. In mathematics and most scientific reading, of course, the opposite is true. In highly technical writing, perhaps with lines on lines of equations, you need to follow *everything* on the page. Thus this chapter applies more to the social sciences and humanities and some professional courses (Chapters 8, 9, and 11) than to the physical sciences (Chapter 10).

Purchasing Tips
For some classes you may get away with not buying the textbook; other students can give you guidance here. Some books are outrageously expensive, and creative alternatives may be the smarter way to go. Is it online somewhere? Could I borrow it from someone who's completed the course, or share with another student? If you're deciding on a book purchase, check the back cover and the table of contents. Read the conclusion, flip through some of the middle pages, and decide whether this is a good buy. Even when books are assigned, we are not victims. There are ways to make the best of the book, rather than allowing the book to get the better of us!

Skimming Tips
Reading a longer book is in some ways like a treasure hunt. A good map will lead you to that buried chest. There is no need to traverse every inch of ground on the map, only the parts essential to reaching your goal.

Considering all the material you have to cover, do you really believe you're expected to know every detail of every book, or that it's essential to read every word to get the main points? A 300-page book might have five or ten points worth remembering—but certainly not 100! To find these choice nuggets, we need to master the art of skimming.

- Always read introductions, first and last chapters, and conclusions rather than charging into a book indiscriminately. Read these sections *thoroughly*. It's unfortunate that most readers skip prefaces and introductions, whereas these often contain the most important material![12]

- Skim the remaining pages. In every chapter, read the first paragraph or introduction, and the last paragraph or conclusion.

- For the bulk of the chapter, look for the main sentence in each paragraph. In any well-written work, there will be one main idea. (That's the purpose of paragraphing.) Skim till you locate it. You'll see that it usually comes first, though it may end up at the paragraph's conclusion.

- Don't overdo it—it's too tiring. Be confident. There's no need to be intimidated by the sheer volume of the assigned reading.

- Skimming the book might yield 1–5 pages of notes. Remember, professors want you to grasp main concepts, events, dates, persons etc.—essentials more than peripherals.

General Tips

Several common-sense guidelines will set you up for victory. (Some are repeated from the previous chapter.)

- Read with highlighter and pen available. Don't overdo it; but highlights make it extremely easy to locate the salient points. If you plan to resell your books, perhaps you should use a pencil (and, later, an eraser).

- Have a dictionary handy. If you come across difficult words, look them up. It not only builds your vocabulary, but leads to fuller comprehension of concepts.

- Don't read in a too warm a room. If you have no choice,

have a cool drink or a cup of ice on hand.

- Don't read with music in the background unless the music is without words. Never study with a television or other monitor on unless it's a necessary part of your assignment. These slow most students down.[13] You may enjoy studying more, but you will retain less and spend hours longer than necessary in your books.

- Squeeze reading into the idle moments, like while you're exercising (e.g. on an elliptical machine) or waiting for someone at the airport. It's amazing how much extra time can be wrung from your week!

- Perhaps have more than one book (subject) on your table. Alternating lessens fatigue; variety stimulates.

- Don't read too long without a break. You may find that twenty, forty, or sixty minutes is your maximum before you hit diminishing returns! *Schedule* these breaks. (Remember "the fallacy of the sponge" from the last chapter.)

- Take time to review your highlights within a day or two of finishing the book.

- If you've never read *How to Read a Book: The Classic Guide to Intelligent Reading,* by Mortimer J. Adler and Charles Van Dorn, let me strongly recommend this volume. Most of us equate reading ability with literacy. Of course we need to know our ABCs and be able to read English, but in university this is not what is meant by reading. It's *how* we approach the material that determines whether or not we profit and, in the case of college classes, whether we learn more and receive a better grade as a payoff for the hours we invest in a book. The common reaction to *How to Read a Book* is: "I didn't think I needed this book, but am I ever glad I took your advice! I'm 18 (22, 30...) years old, but in all these years no one ever taught me *how* to read!" It's a purchase you will not regret.

Required Reading
- If possible, purchase books well ahead of time. Aim to become familiar with them during breaks or vacation times.

Pay attention to the back cover, reviewers' comments, and introductions.

- If you leave purchasing or ordering a book too late, you may succeed in locating a digital version.

- Used books are a strong consideration for those on limited budgets.

- Speak with students who have completed your course. Ask them which parts of the required reading seemed to receive greatest emphasis in lectures and exams.

- If the author of the text is your professor, pay special attention. Be sure to ask him/her about any features you are having trouble comprehending. Show respect to the author and remember, come exam time, that teachers rarely withhold credit from those who agree with their own views. Be sincere (disingenuous), but also wise.

- In smaller classes or seminars, do some reading in the *recommended* as well as the *required* category. This will enhance your class participation, add depth to essays, and build rapport with professor and students.

- Make an effort to complete required reading well before exam time.

Certainly we want to do neither more nor less work than is really necessary. These pointers should make your reading more enjoyable and your degree more profitable.

---

[12] As an author, I often put my introductory material into chapter 1, so that my readers don't miss it.

[13] Watching an hour of TV after the age of twenty-five can shorten the viewer's life by just under twenty-two minutes, according to University of Queensland researchers. Smoking two cigarettes has approximately the same effect. The problem is not actually TV itself, but the lack of activity on the part of the viewer for long periods. Cardiovascular disease, excess weight, diabetes, and other health problems result from a sedentary lifestyle (MSNBC and Reuters, 8/7/11).

6. PREPARING INTERESTING PAPERS

Most subjects require the writing of papers, whether reflection papers (2 pages), short pieces (3–5 pages), longer ones (10–20 pages), or major works (50 pages). Since any paper competes with other activities for your precious time, wouldn't you like to shave a few hours off your writing time? But before we get to the nitty-gritty, here's a proverb that I have found particularly inspiring.

> *It is the glory of God to conceal a matter;*
> *to search out a matter is the glory of kings (Proverbs 25:2).*

Searching out a matter—research—can be glorious. This single proverb seems to support the research scientist as much as it does the sociologist or historian. If we search out a matter in the right way and with God in mind, we may come to actually enjoy the process.

Okay, back to reality! No one escapes the necessity of writing term papers, so a thought-through strategy will usually yield rich dividends. Our aim: to be better prepared to produce effective papers. The principles are few and simple.

Think Positively!
Never complain about paper assignments. You're learning your subject; your character is being honed; you're putting to use the skills acquired in previous years of study. Besides, once you graduate, what makes you so sure you won't still need to produce reports, papers, or even books? This is an excellent investment in your own future.

Preparation
Don't leave papers to the last minute. You may find source materials in scarce demand or even unavailable. Instead, put your initial thoughts on paper several weeks ahead of time so that, with the assignment in the back of your mind, you will be alert to relevant ideas or materials. Last-minute paper writing puts you under pressure to

take shortcuts. The result is not likely to be glorious.

Sources

Keep complete bibliographic information on any sources you cite. There is absolutely no need to be combing through disordered scraps of paper when you're producing your bibliography or adding the notes. Besides, if you're sloppy, you're more likely to cite without attribution, or worse, incorporate someone else's work as your own words (plagiarism). I've found it's easiest to create footnotes or end-notes as soon as I've used the source. Programs like Microsoft Word make this a cinch. Give credit wherever possible—credit for ideas as well as for citations. The greater the number of sources, the more it will seem you have done your homework. Avoid quoting writers quoting other writers! Work, as far as possible, with original sources.

Grammar

These days, English standards are low. What used to be expected before a student entered high school is now optional, and there are millions of college grads who read and write only at a fourteen-year-old level.[14] Every year I serve as an adjunct professor for a couple of months, and I require my master's degree students to submit papers. No more than 10 or 20% of them have acceptable English skills; many papers are riddled with errors. So, if English isn't your strong suit, check over each paragraph you've written to ensure it makes sense and that you haven't "invented" vocabulary or whacky grammar. Even if there are scores of corrections to be made, the time will be well worth the higher grade.

Vocabulary

Don't try to sound too clever! Don't be sesquipedalian, and don't use words about whose meanings you are not certain. Clarity is always to be valued over grammatical or verbal flourishes. On the other hand, avoid using the same words over and over again. Synonyms well uti-lized make reading a pleasure.

Format

Most professors prefer that your paper be double spaced. Boldfaced subheads break up the text and make for easier reading. Where possible, insert charts, graphs, and tables. A blank page at the end of the paper affords space for teachers' comments. Page numbers are always helpful to the reader. Inserting the paper into an attractive binder may also be worth a few points. (External presentation isn't everything, but it does make an impression.) Don't staple too close to the text; a single diagonally positioned staple in the top left corner is usually most effective.

Length
If your paper is too long, there are three ways to shrink it. Firstly, there is the rewrite. Secondly (and more simply) there is the possibility of selecting the entire piece of text and altering font size—easily accomplished with today's word processing software. If your professor requires a standard format (like 12 point Times New Roman with 1-inch margins all round), however, that won't work. A third means of reducing the length is the inclusion of larger blocks of text in foot- or endnotes. This also lends a more professional or scholarly appearance to your work. If the paper is too short, on the other hand, you can expand print size, change the margins, or bring some of your notes into the text. Make sure that the introduction/conclusion clearly state/restate your position.

Color
Ask yourself the honest question: Does this paragraph have a dull feel to it? If so, rewrite. Is it too heavy, or lacking in conviction? Make sure some of the color of your personality comes through in your writing.

Proofread!
Finally, before you turn in your masterpiece, carefully proofread everything. Don't submit your first draft. You might have a friend (one who knows how to disagree or give frank input) check your paper over for clarity, grammar, and style. Allow time for revision—don't write off the top of your head without adequate

---

[14] The NIV Bible, the bestselling translation in the English world, is pitched towards those who read at the standard of grade 8.5. Versions like the New King James or the New American Standard, in contrast, are suitable for those reading at an 11th-grade level—sadly, the minority of adults.

7. EXCELLING IN EXAMINATIONS

In our last chapter on academic skills, we'll address the dreaded exam. In this chapter we'll progress from general test strategies to tips on essay writing to tips on answering multiple-choice questions.

GENERAL

Scheduling
A well-organized faculty will inform students of examination dates well ahead of time. Make sure you write into your planning book not only the exam times and dates, but also the dates on which you will need to begin preparing for each exam. There is never any reason to be caught off guard or to be out of breath. Simply schedule wisely.

Arrival
Make sure to come to the exam center early. Eat something beforehand, and get plenty of fluids. Fatigue or lightheadedness from low blood sugar may cost you during exam time. If you might need the restroom, allow time for that as well. Don't answer the phone in the final minutes before the exam. Allow your brain a moment of calm.

Bring two writing implements to the test, in case one fails you. Choose a seat you're happy to spend one, two, or three hours in. Sit up, don't slouch. Greet the professor or proctor. Pray for a clear mind. (The Lord may answer that prayer—though it's doubtful he'll bless those praying to him for recall of something they never studied!)

Priorities
The exam strategy is simple. (1) Read through the entire exam before beginning work. This will enable you to allocate sufficient time to each section, so that you're not rushed at the end. (2) Answer the easiest questions first. This builds confidence as well as momentum. (3) Reserve the remaining time for the harder questions. In this way you may even beat out the brighter students! If you complete the whole exam early, then it's always a good idea to check your work.

How Much to Study?
Over-studying and under-studying are both to be avoided. Ask fellow students how much time they are putting into preparation. Everyone has his or her own pace. When you have studied thoroughly, you will be able to anticipate likely exam questions. Mock exams with fellow students may help. If there is an area or subject you're confused by, don't gloss it over; ask questions and get answers until you're satisfied.

Mental Tricks
In the preparation phase, use mental outlines and construct them in such a way that you can remember them. Mnemonic devices are especially handy. You strongly suspect your psych prof will ask you to compare and contrast some of the most eminent psychologists. You know a fair deal about Jung, Freud, Adler, Rogers, Maslow, and Skinner, though not so much about the others. A possible mnemonic is J-FARMS, using the first letter of each of the six persons. It doesn't matter that the mnemonic is a bit silly (what's a J farm?). All that matters is that it allows ready recall.

Or let's say you've got a test in history. Well-positioned adverbs lend structure to your writing, especially when you place them in parallel (economically/socially/politically/culturally). Or maybe the chem test is a bear, and you can hardly remember the formulas. In this case, keep repeating to yourself the formula for, say, caffeine: $C^8H^{10}N^4O^2$. Before you even open the test, pencil the formula somewhere on the cover the second the teacher says, "You may begin." If and when you need the formula for caffeine—as opposed to feeling you need more caffeine!—no problem. It's already written down! One less thing to keep in your head. This will allay some of the anxiety you feel, especially if you're not a math-science sort of person. The less anxious and the more relaxed you are, the better you are likely to perform. Such devices served me well in high school. I'm sure you have your own bag of tricks.

ESSAYS

Many tests include essay questions, especially in smaller college classes. There is more to preparation than just knowing your stuff, essential as that is. There's a knack to essay writing.

10 Tips on Essay Writing

- Read the question carefully. Often the professor's wording of the question contains a possible outline for your essay.

- Write a brief outline on scratch paper before you launch into the essay. Ensure that you've thought the structure through. If you have a mental outline already in your head, write it out as soon as the exam officially begins.

- Write legibly. Even if this is not possible, at least do your best. Don't write at a severe slant. This irritates the graders. Drawing faint, parallel pencil lines on the paper may help.

- Write in clearly recognizable paragraphs. Once you've begun a new thought, it's time for a new paragraph.

- Locate the sentence containing your point either at the beginning or at the end of the paragraph.

- Subheadings can break up the text and make it more visually appealing.

- If you make a mistake, cross it out discreetly. Avoid the heavily edited look (marks, arrows, carets, text scribbled in margins).

- Concentrate on your opening and your conclusion—the two parts of the essay that create or leave the strongest impression.

- Once finished saying what you want to say, bring the essay to a close. Don't even appear to be droning on!

MULTIPLE CHOICE

10 Tips on Multiple Choice Questions

- Skim over all the questions first.
- Answer with your first thought—which will usually be correct. Don't second-guess yourself (or the teacher). This seldom goes well.

- Find out whether guessing hurts your score. (Is a blank answer scored the same as an incorrect answer?)
- Skip the hard questions; there will be plenty of time at the end, and this practice gives a psychological advantage.
- Don't search too hard for patterns. For example, there are four Bs in a row. Does this mean (1) the next answer must be a B, or (2) that the next answer is highly unlikely to be a B? Don't go there.
- Don't be too clever. They don't make tests like that. Unfortunately, this hurts the truly creative student, who often sees possibilities not envisioned by the test designers.
- Some of the multiple choice answers may seem extreme or extraneous—often one in four will be. Eliminate these first. Usually you will be choosing between one answer that's almost right and the one that is right.
- If in doubt, try to recall the emphasis, words, and even phrasing of teacher. "How would she have put this?"
- Double check all answers. Did you accidentally skip a word? (Did you miss the italicized *not*?)
- In the final minutes, dwell on trickier questions. Don't become panicked or disheartened if you're uncertain.
- Push yourself. Don't dawdle, but proceed at a determined pace.

Yes, exam technique can be perfected! Hopefully you'll anticipate your next exam opportunity as just that—an *opportunity* to hone your skills and, in some way, do your personal best. You'll be asked to take exams of one sort or another for the rest of your life (job applications, driving tests, first aid qualification, continuing education credits, and more). Keep those skills sharp.

Conclusion
We all have different academic abilities, and *attitude* is certainly more important than *aptitude*, yet for every student, academics are a vital part of "spiritual" life. If we're drooping in motivation, we must learn to work for God, not for self, nor even for our professors. Christ is he whom we serve (Col 3:22–23).

III. ENGAGEMENT

"Some students drink at the fountain of knowledge. Others just gargle."   —Unknown

All students are under pressure: from the quantity and difficulty of material to be mastered; from self-doubt in the face of the seniority of teachers, from peer pressure, from pressure to be politically correct, and of course from the ticking clock. Christian students face one additional challenge: pressure to buy in to the world's messages—its lies. In the classroom, we may feel we have little to say.

Fortunately, the Lord is stronger—and smarter—than all the pressures in our lives. Let's use our imagination. What if *Jesus* were taking Psychology 101? What would he say? What comments might he make in your history class? Would he remain silent in New Testament class, or speak up? If he stopped the mouths of the elders when he was twelve, just imagine his interactions as an eighteen-year-old freshman, or a twenty-two-year old graduate student!

CORE AREA 1
EVANGELISM/IMPACT ON CAMPUS

CORE AREA 2
ACADEMICS/GETTING THE GRADES

CORE AREA 3
ENGAGEMENT/USING YOUR MIND

CORE AREA 4
FOLLOW-THROUGH/YOUR NEXT LIFE STAGE

God turns secular wisdom upside down—humanistic thinking promoting inconsistent or even irrational positions. He has made foolish the wisdom of the world (1 Cor 1:20). To have the mind of Christ, we can think strategically about each course *before* the term starts. To help you to prepare, in Section III we will explore inconsistencies, turn bogus arguments inside out, and share interesting facts related to many university courses.[15] You will also find advice for over forty specific classes.

The core value here is *engagement*. The idea isn't just to survive our classes, but to take them *as Christians*—to think like Christ.

Note: The thoughts expressed in "Engagement" are hardly all mine. Although I've taken classes—or at least read heavily—in the majority of disciplines touched on below, I hardly consider myself an expert. My aim has been *broad familiarity* rather than precise technical knowledge. Where I've been uncertain, I've dug deeper and consulted more widely. Much of the material below has been run past experts in their fields.

---

[15]   Of course secular wisdom isn't all wrong. Not all classes are inimical to our faith—the principles of engineering or mathematics hardly undermine or disprove God. Yet even in such classes there are a few key points to keep in mind so that we maintain our spiritual footing. It's a matter of blending, balance, and priorities.

8. SOCIAL SCIENCES

Scores of classes fall under the heading of social sciences. Even if your specific class doesn't show up in this chapter, there may be helpful pointers for a related class. Take a look so you don't miss something relevant to your situation.[16]

In this chapter we will consider nine areas: anthropology, archaeology, economics, geography, history, linguistics and languages, political science, psychology, and sociology. Because of the volume of material, all comments are bullet points.

Anthropology
- Anthropologists on the whole tend to have a troubled relationship with religion. Some reduce religion and the perception of the numinous to something less disturbing.[17] In class discussions, you may need to encourage professors and fellow students to be open-minded. Challenging a belief without first seeking to understand the person (getting to know them) may come off as abrasive, so speak in such a way that the other person feels your respect and personal warmth.
- What does it mean to be human? It is clear that there were thousands of generations of prehumans before man arrived on the scene. The question of whether Adam and Eve are literal persons (or are representative of mankind) is really a moot point. At *some* point *homo sapiens* appeared on planet earth—humans, created in the image of God.
- Romans 2:12–16 reminds us that those who haven't received the word of God will not thereby evade God's judgment. Religious or irreligious, monotheist or polytheist, the whole world has a sin problem, and none will be saved apart from the gospel of Jesus Christ. It is interesting to note that virtually all other religions posit that only personal good works can save man and allow him to find paradise, however it is defined.
- European missionary impact was *not* all negative, nor were societies before contact with (some form of) Christianity a pristine

utopian paradise. They were sinful. They abused the environment. They enslaved their neighbors. Many practiced human sacrifice. Margaret Mead is typical of those who romanticize people groups before contact with the Europeans. She depicted Samoan culture as "a paradise of free love,"[18] ignoring the negative effects of sin and promiscuity among the Samoans.

- Anthropologists of religion often commit the *genetic fallacy*: the belief that determining the origin of an idea (or religion) explains away the idea. This will not work. While it is true that those born in Tibet will likely be Buddhists, and those in Mississippi, Baptists, the correlation has no connection to the truth or falsehood of their beliefs. In fact, scholars who seek to relativize all religions in this way cut the ground from under their own feet. If we know that an anthropologist's worldview was influenced by her liberal education in New England, her parents' divorce, and a bad experience with a Bible-banger, we're not at all surprised that she turned out to be atheist or agnostic. That doesn't necessarily mean, however, that her view is wrong (though I think it is). Ideas must be examined on their own merits, not accepted or dismissed because of the way in which their proponents acquired them.

- Anthropology sheds light on what it is to be human and reminds us that humans are naturally religious animals. It also illuminates the ways in which people search for meaning—which reminds us that we do not inhabit the absurd world of the existentialists, but a planet brimming with curiosity and thought.

Archaeology

- For Christians, archaeology is an important field. Since the Bible is primarily a book of relationships (God, neighbor, friend, family, enemies), and this discipline takes us back in time, the snapshots it provides of ancient cultures remind us that *their* concerns aren't all that different from our own. On the whole, they had the same problems and hopes that we do, for example, marriage, children, cuisine, taxation, social organization, art, worship, and the afterlife.

- Archaeology in the biblical lands (most of which are clustered around the eastern end of the Mediterranean) lends color to the biblical story and reminds us all that the story is rooted in real history and geography.[19]

- Critics of the Bible have often been refuted by archaeological discoveries. For example, those who denied the existence of the Hittites had to eat their words once evidence of this powerful empire turned up around the turn of the previous century. More recently, claims that there is no evidence of Pontius Pilatus other than mention in the Bible was refuted when, in 1961, the "Pilate stone" was unearthed at the archaeological site of Caesarea Maritima. In 2009 the first-century synagogue at Magdala—as in Mary Magdalene—was unearthed, the seventh in Israel to date. Until recently radical scholars denied that there were any synagogues in first-century Israel!

- Only a small portion of the Holy Land has been excavated, so much more is likely to turn up and fill in some of the gaps in our understanding.[20]

- Yet for the most part, archaeology doesn't so much *prove* the Scriptures as *illustrate* them.

- It seems the early Christian may not have shared our appreciation for archaeology. Ever since the fourth century AD there has been a lucrative business surrounding manufactured relics, leading to Christian pilgrimage. In the first few centuries there seems to have been little if any interest in visiting the Holy Land. Once it became a business, thousands of relics began to be "discovered" (the true Holy Cross, for example).

- Beware hoaxes and unproved assertions, like the discovery of Noah's Ark, the Ark of the Covenant, Pharaoh's drowned army, Nephilim skeletons, and so on. Don't believe everything on the Internet. Serious archaeologists recognize a number of structures and objects related to the Bible—and when they do, you can put stock in what they publish. Armchair archaeologists speculate, making claims without proof, and even if their articles seem to confirm the Bible, don't embrace their claims. Most will be, or already have been, refuted.

- Not all finds are bogus—there's still plenty of evidence to illustrate the biblical world.[21]

Economics

- Capitalism at first seems Christian, but the "little guy" is often crushed. Communism at first also seems good, until we realize that the individual is often sacrificed for the state.

- Communism doesn't work. It disrupts and even destroys economic prosperity, freedom of speech, happiness, and enterprise. Even if Communism *were* on track, humans are too selfish for such a grand plan to be realistic. It is fair to charge its adherents with an overly rosy view of human nature.

- Watch out for consumerism! Work to eat, eat to work... an endless cycle! Ask, "Where does this lead? Does it satisfy?" (see Eccl 5:10).

- The application of Darwinism to socialism, called social Darwinism, led to a number of failed movements in the 19th and 20th centuries, eugenics and Nazism among them.

- "Religious wars" are normally about money and power. Religion makes for a nice justification. The Crusades were driven by economic concerns on the part of the pope. (Most of those who participated lost money, and not a few were wiped out by the expenses of crusading.)

- "Prosperity theology"—the belief that when we are faithful to God, he causes us to prosper financially and in other areas—contradicts both Scripture and experience.[22] Its favorite proof-text, Jeremiah 29:11–14, fails to prove the tenet that it is the Lord's purpose to make us rich and successful. (The verse immediately before, Jeremiah 29:10, indicates that the promise of a successful return to Israel would not be fulfilled for many decades.) As prosperity theology corrupts the motive to be faithful no matter what, it must be strongly rejected by biblical Christians.

- Christians need to take seriously all the biblical passages on wealth and possessions—which number in the hundreds! Although there is no "Christian economics," the sphere of prosperity and consumption tell a lot about one's faith. Money is the root of all sorts of evil. In this sense, lucre is *dangerous*—a word seldom attached to money, which shows how unaware we are of its beguiling nature, especially in the prosperous nations of the West.

Geography

- Geography should be appreciated by all Christians, since the biblical story takes place in time and *space* (place). Unless we have a general understanding of the geography of the biblical world, many things will slip past us. The story of the Bible feels more concrete, realistic, and real when we are equipped with basic geographical knowledge.

- The Scriptures tell us that God created an earth that would eventually support humans who would seek him (Acts 17:26).[23] The right terrestrial combination of land, sea, and topographic features facilitates the time and energy necessary for seeking God. The way the world is allows us to know the Creator.

- Each geographic location requires different evangelistic strategies. Studying geography is a great way for Christians to learn about various societies and how to bring the gospel into differing cultures.

- When our knowledge of geography is poor, it is harder to be moved by natural disasters or take interest in political events and other conditions that affect our brothers and sisters around the planet.

- Travelling, especially internationally, gives us an edge when it comes to connecting with different kinds of people (1 Cor 9:19–23). If we can't travel, at least we can read, listen, or surf.

- Suggestion: Learn all the national capitals and locations on a map.[24] This is a helpful conversation starter when you meet someone from another country.

History

- History should be appreciated by all Christians, since the biblical story takes place in *time* and space.

- In history teaching at the elementary and secondary level there has been a move away from facts and dates to trends and analysis. Unfortunately, without the solid framework of such data, analysis is simply not possible.[25] For example, without knowing when certain events took place, it is difficult to explore causality: what caused what.

- "The winners write the history books," it is often pointed out. Granted. But does this mean that the relativists are right—that there's no objective truth, no facts that history can lay hold of? Of course not. If there is no objective truth, then it cannot actually be true that there's no objective truth—which is nonsensical.

- Historians try to be value-neutral—yet can anyone study the past without *any* bias? Should we really avoid value judgments? Isn't *that* a value judgment?

- European history is closely intertwined with church history, a lot of which isn't pretty. But hold on! The thread of authentic Christianity was broken way back in the fourth century.[26] As long as the church was purified by persecution, she seems to have been more or less holy. Once persecution ceased, in 311,[27] the persecuted soon became the persecutor. Power corrupted the church. So keep in mind that the institutional church from the Middle Ages is, for the most part, an apostate organization. We should expect compromise, un-Christian behavior, and corruption.

- The Crusades, the Inquisition, and other horrors committed by "Christians" are blights on the church. But wait a minute. Is doing something *in the name of* Christ the same as doing something by his authority? Of course not. Violence is opposed to the teaching of the founder of Christianity (Matt 5:43–48). It may be true that the institutional church or Christendom (the church in close relation to the state) has committed atrocities. Yet it is *not* true that Christ has committed atrocities.

- Just as Christians should strive to know the history of biblical times, both OT and NT, we also benefit by learning the flow of church history. Learn what happened (and why it's important) in 325, 431, 1054, 1099, 1517, and so on. There is much to learn!

- It is profitable to study history, even if only to avoid pitfalls. "Those who cannot remember the past are condemned to repeat it" —George Santayana (1863–1952).[28]

- There are numerous historical documentaries that can bring life and color to your study. Take advantage of them, especially where you feel there's a gap in your knowledge.

Linguistics and Foreign Languages

• Humans are deeply invested in communication. So are animals, though not in the same ways: they don't philosophize; they don't celebrate their achievements; their "languages" are simple and seem devoid of abstract thought. Although humans *are* part of the animal kingdom, they are set apart from their closest relations— even if they share 99% of their genetic material.

• Against the postmodernists, language does not *create* reality. Rather, language is a way of talking about reality.

• Comparative philology suggests all human languages did *not* come from a single common tongue. There are families of languages, and efforts to trace them all back to one protolanguage have failed. This has implications for deciding if Genesis 11:1–9 should be interpreted literally or symbolically.[29]

• See also comments under "Classical Studies."

• Whenever you have the opportunity, read the text *out loud*. Listen to yourself. This will enable you to improve your accent and be more aware of any words you have trouble pronouncing.

• Foreign languages open doors into missionary work. They also make us clearer communicators in our native tongue. Learn your foreign language(s) well.

Political Science

• The Bible has many passages on power, politics, and governance—for example, at least twenty-two in Proverbs.[30]

• The early church was not a commune. Individuals owned private property. Even after Ananias and Sapphira sold their land, they still the money was still theirs. Their sin wasn't that they held back some of their wealth, but that they pretended to be more sacrificial than they really were (Acts 5:4). There were elements of both capitalism *and* socialism in the NT church. (But in both the Old and New Testaments it was acknowledged that ownership was fleeting and everything ultimately belonged to God [Deut 28, 30; Eccl 2:26; Luke 12:19–21]).

• Our citizenship is in heaven (Phil 3:20). This means, among other things, that we cannot pledge *ultimate* allegiance to any earthly power or government.[31]

- Even in secular or atheist states, despite attempts to shut God out of the public square, quasi-religious systems are the usual result. The state (nominally—but actually the leadership) takes the place of God. Yet no person or institution or system has the right to demand our total loyalty—even if, and especially if, the institution is religious in nature. Whenever governments have made exclusive claims over the minds and hearts of their citizens, the natural results have been duplicity, injustice, violence, and a culture of fear. (Think Cambodia, Cuba, or the Soviet Union.)

- Civil disobedience may be occasionally justified. We obey the government except when it contradicts the law of God (Dan 3:18; 6:10). On the other hand, we pay taxes even if they're unfair or we disagree with how the government plans to spend them (Rom 13:6–7). The New Testament stresses ceding our rights for the good of others, not demanding them (Rom 14:1–15:7; 1 Cor 8:1–11:1).

- Beware of politics![32] Power was not Jesus' way of effecting change—and he was offered political kingship (John 6:15; see 18:36).[33] That's why Jesus forbade his followers to behave in an authoritarian manner or use power for coercive purposes (Mark 10:42–45).[34] He also forbade his followers to lord it over others.[35] Lower level positions involve less compromise, but there's extreme temptation to compromise "at the top." Lord Acton (1834–1902) got it right: "Power tends to corrupt, and absolute power corrupts absolutely. Great men are almost always bad men."[36] The modern political arena may be as dangerous a place for Christians as the ancient Roman arena.

- In the Old Testament, the "church" (God's people) and the state (Israel) were one. Yet even then, the king was not allowed to act as a priest, nor were priests allowed to lead the nation.[37] The division of church and politics under the new covenant makes a sharp contrast.

- American citizens: know that when your country was founded, separation of church and state existed at the federal level—much less so at the state level.

- We should pray for our political leaders (1 Tim 2:1–2).

- In the area of politics, we may hold various opinions, as long as we don't cause others to stumble (Rom 14:13) or expressly disrespect political leaders (1 Pet 2:17). Posting strong political opinions at social media sites risks violating these principles, as well as alienating those we should be reaching out to.

Psychology

- Introductory psychology classes are often popular—and easy. Did you sign up in hopes of an "easy A"?
- Psychology comes from two ancient Greek words, *psyche* (soul) and *logos* (study). It's ironic that while many scientists are exploring the brain and the origin of consciousness, there are psychologists who do not even believe humans have a soul—something that lives on. The English word "psyche" has a different meaning now.
- Psychology is a legitimate field. Christians need to appreciate its contributions and learn when to refer those suffering from mental illness to qualified professionals. And yet...
- Most of the counsel that most of us need can come from fellow Christians (Rom 15:14).[38]
- Obeying God, being open with our lives, being industrious not lazy, staying connected with people (not living as a loner)—these are the sorts of things the Bible connects with happiness and spiritual health (Prov 3:7–8; 14:30; 15:13; 17:22; 18:14; 29:6). Any school of psychology that fails to regard the spiritual component will be limited in its ability to maximize the quality of human life.
- When we replace God with any other thing, person, system, ideal, etc., we are left empty. Such things cannot fill the God-shaped void in our hearts (Eccl 3:11).
- When your professor speaks of *dysfunction*, this implies a healthy norm, the way things *should* function. But to make *that* value judgment we need some external standard—otherwise the "norm" ends up being merely an average. As Christians we know that God's plan for healthy, functional relationships (community, family, marriage, friendships) is laid out in the Scriptures.
- Thanks to Freud,[39] words like *sin, wickedness, righteous,* and

virtue are rare among psychologists and psychiatrists. They opine that people aren't *sinful*; they are ignorant. Criminals don't need to be *punished*, but *cured*. Commenting on this trend, in 1973 psychiatrist and author Karl Menninger wrote *Whatever Became of Sin?*

- "Religion is comparable to a childhood neurosis," Freud said.[40] Our world is full of neuroses (psychological disorders): narcissistic personality disorder, anorexia nervosa, bipolar I and II disorder, cocaine dependence, delusions of grandeur, obsessive-compulsive disorder, borderline personality disorder, and many more. We humans tend to be neurotic, so it shouldn't be surprising that some people's religion bears the marks of neurosis. In fact, it would be surprising if those in the church bore none of the marks of broken humanity. But what about the millions of people who are stable and well balanced psychologically who believe in God? Dismissing religion because some of its adherents are neurotic is unreasonable.

- Ought we to live naturally, organically? No, since such a path is nearly impossible to define. In the animal world, there is nothing natural about picking up after oneself. Nor is there anything wrong with one animal attacking another animal and eating it. Many species are sexually promiscuous. Some engage in homosexual acts. There is no moral dimension to such behaviors. And yet the Lord calls us to live above the natural, animal level—the flesh—to live spiritually.

- Premarital sexual experimentation is not beneficial, but destructive.

- There is no "gay" gene. Every behavior is affected by a combination of genes. Brain chemistry may be both a cause and an effect of behavior and emotion.

- In 2011, the average US adult believed that 25% of the population is homosexual, according to a Gallup poll. The tendency to overstate this statistic is reinforced by the liberal media. The actual part of the population that is homosexual is only 2–3%.[41]

- We are more than the sum total of our choices. To understand individual humans, we must also understand culture, brain chemistry and development, family of origin and continued relational patterns, and their spiritual condition. (For more on this, see Appendix B, "Holistic Campus Ministry.")

- Parapsychology has led nowhere. This doesn't constitute a rebuttal of the claim of a supernatural world, only a discrediting of the thousand psychics and clairvoyants who would mislead us.

- Whereas our personality is largely determined by genetics and early childhood relationships, character can be built (Rom 5:1–5). That's good news. The Holy Spirit transforms us—not normally by replacing our personalities, but by making us into persons of character, love, patience, and other Christlike attributes.

- Not only are we better equipped to make disciples when we can comfortably navigate the psyche, but we are more aware of our own schemas and issues. We cannot function more like Jesus until we learn how dysfunctional we are—and how unlike Jesus!

Sociology

- Christians appreciate sociology because sociology is the study of society—its development, structure, function, and trends. And Christians are interested in people!

- Sociologists like Troelstch distinguish between "sect" and "church." The sect, rejecting the world's values, exists in a state of high tension with ambient society. A church, on the other hand, lives in a state of low tension with society; it has bought in to most of its values. (Which are we?)

- The Bible portrays both function and dysfunction. Function: it was the Creator's purpose that one man would be one flesh with one wife for life. Dysfunction: the polygamy tolerated in the Old Testament shows the stress and selfishness that emerge in a polygamous context. Important: the Bible (esp. the Old Testament) often *reports*, but does not *approve*, behaviors that diverge from God's intention.[42]

- Generations ago, the basic social unit was the extended family: grandparents, parents, and children. With the institutionalizing of the elderly, the basic unit became the nuclear family. After the sexual revolution, and almost certainly because of it, the basic family unit is increasingly mother and child—fathers being absent or divorced. This is only a temporary configuration (parents die). And so the basic social unit is well on the way to being *the individual!*

- In Western culture, the traditional family is being redefined. With the majority of children being born to single mothers or couples lacking a marriage commitment, there is a new norm. Normative families, however, aren't necessarily *normal*—they don't tell us how things should be, only how they actually are.

- Western work culture sacrifices the family.[43] The two-income family-cum-daycare system is suboptimal, biblically speaking. All things being equal, children are ideally brought up by two parents: a mother and a father.[44]

- There is ample evidence that cohabitation hurts children and is a bad deal for the mother.[45]

- Columbia University's National Center on Addiction and Substance Abuse finds that teenagers who have dinner with their parents three or fewer times per week are 4x more likely to use tobacco, 2x as likely to drink, and 2.5x more likely to smoke pot as their fellow teens who have dinner with their parents 5–7 times a week.[46]

- Rates of serious child abuse are lower in intact families; six times higher in stepfamilies; 14 times higher in always-single-mother families; 20 times higher in cohabiting biological-parent families; and 33 times higher when a mother is cohabiting with a boyfriend who is not the biological father.[47]

- The National Marriage Project at the University of Virginia has found just 11% of college-educated Americans divorce within the first 10 years of marriage, compared with almost 37% for the rest of the population.[48]

- The number of single mothers in the US has tripled since 1976, and 38% of mothers who gave birth in 2010 were single. In fact, only 27% of American kids live with their biological mother and father.

- A major socializing instrument is the television. A Northwestern University study found that minority youth (age 8–18) spend an average of 13 hours exposed to media a day, nearly five hours more than the average white youth. Asian Americans logged the most media use (13+ hours), followed by Hispanics (13), blacks (just under 13), and whites (8.6 hours/day). Youth 8–18 devote an average 7.65 hours/day to using entertainment media, yet they spend only 16–20 minutes/day on school-focused activities.[49]

---

[16] Admittedly, sometimes the boundary between social sciences and the humanities is fuzzy. and the professions category could subsume almost every category.

[17] "Anthropologists have a reputation for being openly hostile to Christianity. Their antagonism is especially strong for missionaries, who are deemed agents of the West, destroying traditional cultures. But, more than this, anthropologists find it difficult to relate to and understand religion as a whole, even the religions of the cultures they are investigating. As a result they have developed theories of religion that reduce it to functions of cultural arenas they understand better: cognitive uncertainty, psychological need, social unity, political legitimacy, symbolic meaning, and so forth." Eloise Meneses, Professor of Cultural Anthropology, Eastern University, St. Davids, PA, in a review of *The Slain God: Anthropologists and the Christian Faith* (Timothy Larsen) 2014, in *Journal of the American Scientific Association*, Vol.67, No.4, 28 Dec 2015.

[18] Margaret Mead, *Coming of Age in Samoa.*

[19] For several pieces on archaeology, as well as a full-length class on Old Testament archaeology and another on New Testament archaeology, go to http://www.douglasjacoby.com/?s=archaeology.

[20] Highly recommended: Randall Price, *The Stones Cry Out.*

[21] There is always plenty to see on the Biblical Study Tours that I conduct!

[22] Of course there is a *general* relationship between industry and wealth, but there are many exceptions; thousands of faithful believers end up *losing* their prosperity, whether imprisoned for their faith, dying in famine or plague, or suffering at the hands of oppressive crime syndicates or governments.

[23] This passage has nothing to do with predestination, as Calvinists understand it (God predestining us to live at certain addresses and at certain times). This is to make the Lord a micromanager—something he certainly does not seem to be, whether in Scripture or in the processes of nature. Paul seems to be referring to Deuteronomy 32:8 LXX (the Greek translation of the Old Testament made in the centuries immediately before Christ).

[24] One method I have found useful is to print out a world map but with all words left out. Keep only national borders. Then test yourself!

[25] I wonder whether the same illusion is affecting Christians' knowledge of the Bible. If we learned the names, dates, places, and successions of empires, we would

be less bewildered as we read the historical and prophetic books of the Bible. There would also be payoffs for readers of the gospels, Acts, and the epistles.

[26] This is not to say that there were no genuine Christians between the 4th century and the present. I am generalizing.

[27] Roman persecution ended in AD 311, though some continued in parts of the empire till 324, right before the Council of Nicaea (325).

[28] George Santayana, *Reason in Common Sense,* 1906.

[29] After the Flood we find only the languages in the region of the eastern Mediterranean—which is the locus of nearly all the biblical story. At Babel, faith in technology ends in alienation. Babel in several ways is the opposite of Pentecost: linguistic confusion instead of linguistic unity; alienation instead of love; separation instead of coming together.

[30] For example, Proverbs 8:15–16; 11:14; 14:2, 34; 16:10–15; 21:3; 22:16; 25:4–5; 28:2, 12, 15–16, 28; 29:2, 4, 12, 14; 31:4–5.

[31] For more on politics, see the articles and podcasts at http://www.douglasjacoby .com/category/podcasts/various/politics/.

[32] The words of Nietzsche are apropos: "A man who strives after great things, looks upon every one whom he encounters on his way either as a means of advance, or a delay and hindrance—or as a temporary resting-place. His peculiar lofty *bounty* to his fellow-men is only possible when he attains his elevation and dominates..." (*Beyond Good and Evil,* 273, emphasis added). Notice that the philosopher feels he is doing a favor to others by *dominating* them.

[33] Peterson and Stott put it well: "We would do well not to be enamored by the kind of leadership that is so prized by politicians and CEOs, the kind that is conspicuous and, as we say, 'effective.' Forget about charisma, go for character." —Eugene Peterson, *The Unnecessary Pastor*; and "The very first thing which needs to be said about Christian ministers of all kinds is that they are 'under' people (as their servants) rather than 'over' them (as their leaders, let alone their lords). Jesus made this absolutely plain. The chief characteristic of Christian leaders, he insisted, is humility not authority, and gentleness not power." —John Stott, *The Gospel and the End of Time.*

[34] Podcast available: http://www.douglasjacoby.com/lording-others-mark-1042/.

[35] The specific Greek verb is *katakurieuein* (1 Pet 5:1–3; Mark 10:42–45; Matt 20:25–28; also Acts 19:16; Gen 1:28). Listen to the podcast at http://www.douglasjacoby .com/lording-others-mark-1042/.

[36] Letter to Bishop Mandell Creighton, April 5, 1887 published in *Historical Essays and Studies,* edited by J. N. Figgis and R. V. Laurence (London: Macmillan, 1907).

[37] Priests had to come from the tribe of Levi, kings from Judah—a measure that maintained the separation of church and state. The surrounding nations, however, had priest-kings. The Lord in his wisdom separated spiritual and secular power.

[38] On this point Jay Adams (*Competent to Counsel*) is correct—but not in his sim-

plistic view that sin lies at the root of all psychological problems.

[39] Freud was Jewish, though an atheist. At the time the Nazis were taking over Germany, Freud wrote a work critical of the Judeo-Christian faith, *Moses and Monotheism*.

[40] Sigmund Freud, *The Future of an Illusion*, 1927.

[41] Strongly recommended: www.strengthinweakness.org.

[42] For more on the revolutionary nature of God's plan for society, hear http://www.douglasjacoby.com/israel-a-community-of-radical-counter-culture/.

[43] Recommended: Robert Wuthnow, *Poor Richard's Principle*.

[44] According to a twenty-six-year longitudinal study, the strongest factor indicating whether children practiced high levels of empathic concern for others in their adult years was whether they had an involved father in their lives. In fact, father care was a stronger indicator here than the top three other strongest maternal factors combined. Source: *Pastor's Weekly Briefing*, 8/5/11.

[45] See http://www.douglasjacoby.com/q-a-0716-cohabitation-live-in-lovers/. Further,

1. The rate of divorce among those who cohabit prior to marriage is 39% vs. 21% for couples who marry without prior cohabitation. (W. J. Bennett, The Broken Hearth: Reversing the Moral Collapse of the American Family, 2001).
2. Compared to children of married "biological" [I always find that term amusing] parents, children ages 12–17 with cohabiting parents are six times more likely to exhibit emotional and behavioral problems. They are also 122% more likely to be expelled from school and 90% more likely to have a low grade point average (New Oxford Review 9/07).
3. New Oxford Review 9/07.
4. 75% of children involved in criminal activity are from cohabiting households.
5. Cohabiters who never marry have 78% less wealth than the continuously married; cohabiters who have been divorced or widowed once have 68% less wealth (Cohabitation Facts web site).

Other family facts:

1. For the first time, unmarried adults represent more than half of American households, 73% of men and 62% of women in their twenties in 2006 have never been married. Just 23.5% of men and 31.5% of women ages 20–29 were married in 2006 vs. 31.5% of men and 39.5% of women in 2000 (USA Today, 9/12/07).
2. "Men today are far more involved with their families than they have been at virtually any other time in the last century," says Michael Kimmel, author of *Manhood in America: A Cultural History*. In the late 1970s, the average dad spent about a third as much time with his kids as did the average mom. By 2000, that was up to three-fourths. Today men hug their kids more, help with homework more, and tell their kids they love them more. Fathers are

beginning to look more like mothers (Time 10/4/07).

3. More than half of US couples who married in the late 1970s never saw their twenty-fifth anniversary. It's the first time since World War II that married people had a less-than-even chance of still being married twenty-fifth years later. (Christian Post 9/21/07), adapted from "For the Record: The Foster Report" in Christian Counseling Connection (American Association of Christian Counselors, www.AACC.net), vol. 15, issue 4 (2008).

[46] CitizenLink 9/26/11.

[47] *New Oxford Review* 9/07.

[48] CitizenLink 6/22/11.

[49] Christian Post 6/17/11. For more, please see our book *Christian Parenting in a Non-Christian World.*

9. HUMANITIES & THE ARTS

In this chapter we will consider numerous areas usually located in the Humanities Division of your college: architecture, arts (general), arts (performing), arts (visual), classical studies, literature, philosophy, philosophy (ethics), religion (general), religion (Old Testament), religion (New Testament), and religion (world religions). Again, because of the volume of material, all comments are bullet points, with some extra material in the endnotes.

Architecture

- There are many spiritual applications.
    - ° Christ is the "builder" of all (Heb 3:4).
    - ° Our "city with foundations" is built by God (Heb 11:10).
    - ° Paul was a "master builder" in the area of church planting and growth (1 Cor 3:10 ESV).
    - ° We should build our lives on the Word (Matt 7:24–27).
    - ° "Unless the Lord builds the house, the builders labor in vain" (Psalm 127:1).
- The Old Testament has at least one massive building project: the temple.
- Good architecture allows freedom within structure. Still, builders must respect the laws of physics. Even if the beams are hidden from view, they are still necessary.
- The architecture of life (cell biology, DNA, RNA) is mind-boggling and suggests a God.
- Architecture requires patience and attention to minute detail—consider how Moses obediently followed the model for the tabernacle.
- Tip: Keep ego out of it. Many buildings lack elegance or are inefficiently designed because some architect was overly fond of his blueprints, sacrificing utility, beauty, or both to the expression of some personal "statement." Don't become one of those kinds of architects!

Arts (General)

- The Bible makes clear that artistic gifts are from God (Exodus 31:1–11; 35:10, 25; 35:30–36:2; 36:8; 1 Chr 15:22; 25:7; 2 Chr 2:7–8,13–14; 34:12). If they can be used *spiritually,* then it is true that we possess *spiritual* gifts. Their purpose is to serve others.

- Beauty is real. There are a number of things that transcend the material world (like love, God, and justice).

- When beauty is rejected, or art falls to subjectivism, the result can be absurd, random, or even ugly. Consider atonal music, such as that of John Cage (1912–1992). In rebelling against order and the accepted canons of acoustic beauty, Cage developed anti-music. Is art that appears to be anti-art truly artistic?

- Art reflects one's worldview.[50] Some artists imagine a world without absolutes, one without God. In this case, anything goes. One is reminded of Andres Serrano's award-winning *Piss Christ* (1987), a plastic crucifix submerged in a glass of Serrano's urine.

- Watch out! Artistic license must not morph into moral license! (This is a common theme among the false teachers of Jude and 2 Peter 2–3.) Christ came to set us free, yes, but not "free" in the sense many artists understand it. Firstly, there are always limitations, whether one is a king or a slave. Second, there is no such thing as absolute freedom. Third, the licentious lifestyle of so many in the arts is not freedom as Christ offers it, for sin enslaves! (John 8:34). God calls us to be transformed by the renewing of our minds, not conformed to the thinking of the world (Rom 12:1–2).

- "Freedom of expression" sounds like a good thing. Yet aren't there healthy limits on how we express ourselves? "Freedom of speech" is a political concept permitting the governed to critique the governor, not an absolute right to reject authority, truth, beauty, etc.

- Sensitivity can be both a strength and a weakness. Aesthetic perception is a wonderful thing (I wish I had it). Yet if we're so sensitive that we can't bear to receive critique or can't forgive wrongs, then we're hypersensitive.[51]

Arts (Performing)

- E.g. dance, music, theater.
- We don't have *two* selves in the arts, any more than we do as workers in another field. An accountant ordered to "cook the books" cannot plead that he was only following orders—that it was not *he*, but his boss, who committed wrongdoing. A government agent ordered to commit an assassination cannot excuse himself, "It wasn't *me* doing the killing; it was the government doing it through me." Since there is a unity of person and character, we ought not to do anything on stage that would be immoral to do at home.
- Since we are one person, not two,
  - ° *Pretending* to hate or lust is little different from hating and lusting.
  - ° If we go through the motions of immoral words and deeds, then we will also harbor immoral thoughts.
  - ° Further, we ought never to influence others to do wrong or violate their conscience (Luke 17:1–2; Rom 14:13–23).
- Christians in theater, watch out! This is one of a number of dangerous professions—where you are pressured to compromise or are constantly surrounded by temptation. Similar temptations affect those in professional sports, politics, and other fields. Public figures must pay special attention to their private life.
- Christians in dance, the biblical teaching on modesty still applies (1 Tim 2:9; 1 Cor 12:23; 1 Pet 3:3–4).
- Contrary to the opinion of some fundamentalist groups, dancing isn't unbiblical. There's plenty of dancing within the pages of the Bible, in Old Testament and New Testament alike (Ps 149:3; Eccl 3:4; Luke 15:25). The only bad dance in the New Testament is the one that led to the decapitation of John the Baptist (Mark 6:22). The problem with dance is the *lust* it can incite, when sexual motion, dress, and innuendo conspire to engender lasciviousness. Modest dancing isn't an oxymoron; I have witnessed it numerous times, including in church.
- If you sense that you're beginning to struggle spiritually, consider dropping this class (or major).

Arts (Music)

- Music is a fundamental mode of human expression, and a wonderful way to convey stories, including the biblical narrative and its many subnarratives. Not surprisingly, it is found in every section of the Bible, from the Law to the Prophets to the Psalms to the Gospels to the rest of the New Testament.

- The Psalms were originally sung to a plucked instrument, especially a harp, lyre, or lute. *Psallein* in ancient Greek meant to pluck. In modern Greek it is the word for sing. In NT times the word seems to have already lost its instrumental connotation (as in Eph 5:19).

- Music soothed a troubled king (1 Sam 16:23), got a prophet into a mood receptive to the Spirit of God (2 Kings 3:15), and frequently conveyed joy and sadness alike (the entire Psalter).

- In the course of church history, many times secular tunes have found their way into the church, including many of our most beloved traditional hymns. Initial resistance gave way to ambivalence and finally to acceptance.

- Similarly, despite initial resistance, "contemporary" worship songs were incorporated into the hymnody of the church. The cycle repeats at least once a century. Thus hymn selection doesn't come down to a choice between traditional and contemporary—in the long run it's *both*!

- Some very conservative Christians feel that it is wrong to use instruments during worship, despite the fact that the Old Testament commanded their use, and the New Testament does not prohibit their use.[52]

- As with all the other artistic media, music can convey noble and pure and virtuous thoughts. But when sin enters the scene, music can stimulate base, lewd, violent, or dehumanizing thinking. Let all things be done to the glory of God. "So whether you eat or drink or whatever you do, do it all for the glory of God. Do not cause anyone to stumble, whether Jews, Greeks or the church of God—even as I try to please everyone in every way" (1 Cor 10:31–33).

Arts (Visual)

- E.g. painting, sculpture, film.
- See the caveats for the performing arts (above).
- Based on what we see in God's creation, we may justly conclude that he is an artist.
- Because God created it, the physical world is good—"very good" (Gen 1:31). This is opposite to the view of the Greek philosophers, for whom the material world is inferior, the abstract world of ideas being ultimate reality.
- Jews and Christians have always believed it is permitted to portray physical beings, as long as we don't worship them. Not so in Islam, which misunderstands the taboo on images, forbidding the portrayal of persons or animals in religious art. This leaves the Muslims with geometric patterns, excerpts from the Qur'an, and other aniconic images.
- Beauty isn't just something in the eye of the beholder. We may disagree on *what* is beautiful or ugly, but we must agree that beauty and ugliness exist. When we make ourselves the arbiters of reality, we are in serious existential and spiritual trouble.
- Pornography may incorporate some artistic elements, but it fails as art. True art—beautiful, pure art—ennobles the soul and sets us free to think differently. Pornography hurts both the viewer and the viewed. The viewer is enslaved by sexual addiction; the viewed is treated as an object, discarded once her or his "beauty" has faded. Pornography goes hand in hand with prostitution, sex trafficking, pedophilia, and other blights on society.
- If you sense that you are beginning to not do well spiritually, consider dropping this class (or major).

Classical Studies

- Classics scholars study the Classical Age of Greece and Rome, whose standards and ideals continue to inspire Western civilization, even two millennia later. Similarly, Christians study the "classical" period of the early church (AD 30–325) in order to stay rooted and faithful to apostolic teaching.
- There are many payoffs to studying Latin and Greek.[53] We are

better language students. We're more in touch with our own culture. It makes reading English a simpler and richer experience. And of course, ancient Greek is superb preparation for reading the New Testament in the original tongue.

- Mythology plays a valuable role by providing a backdrop against which the purity and holiness of the one God stand out in stark contrast with the selfishness and capriciousness of the Greco-Roman deities.

- Keep in mind that the classical philosophers—especially Socrates, Plato, and Aristotle—condoned a number of behaviors a Christian would find immoral, from slavery to pedophilia.

- Manuscript evidence for biblical books compares favorably to evidence for the classics.

- Study tip: For Greek and Latin, invest sufficient time into learning conjugations and declensions.

Literature

- Appreciating theme and plot in literature helps us to appreciate the biblical *story*.

- Reading good literature helps us to see the great (and common) themes of human experience, whether tragic or happy, in the Bible—and vice versa. Many great themes of literature are biblical: fall, grace, and redemption; trust, betrayal, revenge, and reconciliation; death and rebirth; death and resurrection.

- Parts of the Bible are fine literature—though other parts are unpolished. Yet the Bible, unlike other ancient works, is not primarily to be studied as literature. We are to discern its story, find the way of God, and orient our lives in that direction.

- One reason Paul was effective is that he was familiar with the literature of the Greco-Roman world, as well as with the literature of Judaism. There is a time for "insider talk," yet there are also times to engage outside culture. We don't have to accept pagan literature in order to understand it, nor does referring to it in our outreach mean we believe it's inspired.

- Every language has poetry. Most biblical poetry is in the Old Testament Whereas in English poetry lines often rhyme ("violets are blue... and I love you"), in Hebrew poetry it is *thoughts* that "rhyme." Generally, the second line parallels the first—synonymously, antithetically, or synthetically.[54]

- Tip: Read each book in full; try to avoid skimming or relying on summaries. Know what you're talking about.

Philosophy

- What is truth? It isn't just opinion (subjective), nor is it mere information (data without context), but something absolute.

- Ours is not a meaningless universe. What is truly unlikely is that, in a meaningless world, it would occur to any thinking being to search for meaning. What could be the source of such a search— unless there *is* meaning?

- Atheism is epistemologically bankrupt. Christians have a better reason for being able to trust in reason, since they believe that the brain (although imperfect) is designed by the Creator to apprehend reality—adequately, though not perfectly. Yet what warrant does an atheist have for assuming that his brain, only the end product of a long evolutionary process, correctly perceives reality?

- Postmodernism claims that reality is socially constructed. Then isn't *this* claim itself also "socially constructed"? So why should we accept it? The claim is incoherent.

- Since all of us should love wisdom (*deî hēmâs sophían phileîn*) all are, in some sense, philosophers!

Philosophy (Ethics)

- All forms of immorality hurt others.[55]

- In desiring to live free from God's authority, our world is trying to replace virtue with "values." But "values" are subjective; you prefer or approve a certain behavior. Your value isn't right or wrong—although it may be "right" for you. No wonder, loosed from its moral moorings, the human race is adrift in a sea of relativity (Eccl 7:29).[56]

- "God is dead and we have killed him," wrote Friedrich Nietzsche (1844–1900). Nietzsche's famous dictum doesn't mean that God once existed but now lives no more. "God is dead" refers to the functional significance of God for morality and ethics. In a god-less world, there is no true morality.[57]

- Nietzsche's predictions for the twentieth century were spot on. He foresaw that the world, morally unhinged, would go crazy, ending up awash in blood. And that's what happened. A pall of insanity descended on our planet, and the levels of violence we reached—often justified by godless or atheistic ideologies—dwarfed all pre-vious centuries (100–200 million deaths).

- Note: Christians do not claim that an atheist can't act morally, or that only Christians are good people. Rather, no one can be moral in a world without morality—and that is the only world possible if there is no God.

- The moral argument for God's existence is one of the most per-suasive, because it's nearly impossible to avoid drawing moral conclusions as we view the world of humanity.[58]

- The Euthyphro Dilemma[59] is easily solved, if the true God is the biblical deity. Good is good not because of any decree, or because good exists apart from the Deity, but because it conforms with God's nature. No command is needed to make something right or wrong (although we do benefit from God's wisdom revealed in his word).

- Intellectuals often appear not to have been able to live virtuous lives by their own philosophies. Hume was a playboy. Rousseau abandoned his children. Nietzsche went insane. "By their fruits you will know them" (Matt 7:20 NKJV).

Religion (General)

- The gods of mythology are inferior to the Judeo-Christian God. Compare them.

- Interpretation is important. Those who reject a view with "That's just your interpretation," are copping out. *Of course* what we un-derstand is our interpretation. And so is the view expressed by the fellow copping out. The question is whether our interpretation is correct. There are right and wrong interpretations.

- Bible scholars fall on a spectrum from conservative to liberal.

  - *Ultraconservative* – The Bible is the word of God, and must be taken literally. Theology is suspect. Biblical training is unnecessary; anyone with a good heart can read and understand Scripture. Obedience is expected. Conservative political positions are the norm.

    o   *Conservative* – The Bible is the word of God. Recognizing the various styles of literature in the Bible, the Scriptures are interpreted literally or metaphorically on literary grounds. Obedience is expected. Conservative political positions are the norm.

    o   *Moderate* – Takes the strong points from both conservative and liberal positions.

    o   *Liberal* – The Bible contains the word of God. Progressive political positions are the norm. Emphasis is placed on individual freedom and expression.

    o   *Ultraliberal* – Although the biblical books are special to Jews and Christians, other scriptures are special to adherents of their religions. We mustn't be judgmental. Salvation is for everyone. (Atheists among the ultraliberal may speak of "salvation" in this life only.) Progressive political positions are the norm.

- Religions are human attempts to make sense of the world by connecting with the gods. In the Bible, God is the one who takes the initiative, not us (Rom 8:28–30; Eph 1:4–5; 1 John 4:10). From the Garden to the Apocalypse, he is the one seeking us. Yet he does not coerce.[60]

Religion (Miracles)

- Miracles are impossible by definition only if we define them that way. There's no reason miracles would have to violate natural law. It may well be that God accelerates natural processes, or works around his laws. Where nonbelievers see miraculous "coincidences," believers feel the hand of God at work and see providence.

- Reality is composed of two "stories." The downstairs is the empirical world, subject to the examination of science. The upstairs is the invisible, nonphysical, spiritual world. There is ample evidence for the reality of both.

- Premodern people weren't stupid; they did not passively accept all miraculous claims. For instance, they knew as well as we do that people don't walk on water—but God might (Matt 14:25; Job 9:8).
- In the Bible there is plenty of evidence that miracles failed to move people whose minds were already made up.

Religion (Old Testament)

- It is important for Christians to know how the testaments fit together. Not only does this afford a panoramic view of sacred history; it also keeps us from errors arising through indiscriminate reading.[61]
- The biblical story isn't the sort of story anyone would just make up. Why would the Hebrews pretend their ancestors were slaves? Or that their most illustrious leader was an adulterer? Similarly, if the church were fabricating the Bible, why the spiritual immaturity of the apostles? Few growth strategies would have been less promising than showcasing the disgraceful death of their founder. And yet that's precisely what the early Christians did (1 Cor 1:23)—and it was powerful!
- Don't get hung up on dating issues. The Old Testament is a compound document and has many layers. The earliest strata go back to the late second millennium BC. Since it is a *collection* of books, all written at different times, it is not important, or even possible, to nail down a single date of composition.
- Liberal scholars typically deny predictive prophecy, routinely dating the prophecy *after* the event it "predicts."
- Not only is the Old Testament a multipart collection, but many of the OT books have multiple authors. For example, Isaiah 8 refers to the disciples of Isaiah who were responsible for writing at least part of Isaiah. Baruch was Jeremiah's scribe, as we see in Jeremiah 36. Here we also note the flexibility of writing, as the second version of the document destroyed by Jehoiakim contains the same message though with somewhat different words. Plurality of sources doesn't disqualify content.
- Genesis 1–11 is generally considered unhistorical by scholars. You may prefer to think of this material as prehistoric, with the

mainstream of Old Testament history beginning with Abraham (Gen 12). Further, the primeval narrative is a different genre. Ancient stories and themes have been reworked in order to make theological points about God and humans. Don't get into arguments about Adam or Noah. Until you are familiar with the background parallel material you will be outclassed.

- Moses crossed the Sea of Reeds (literally, Hebrew *yam suph*). In ancient times the northern extension of the Red Sea, even farther inland than the Gulf of Suez, into the area known as the Sea of Reeds, was sometimes referred to as the Red Sea. When the Jews translated the Old Testament into Greek (the LXX) they used the phrase "Red Sea." Thus you will see both phrases in the text or notes of your Bible.

- Many numbers are figurative. Note, for example, the recurrence of the number forty, for example in the life of Moses or in the book of Judges.

- Idealized ages appear in the earliest strata of the Old Testament. In Genesis 5 there are impossible longevities—if taken literally. Yet the numbers are symbolic, in addition to being based on the Babylonian sexagesimal system (based on the number 60).[62] That is, persons might have *two* ages, one actual and the other ideal. The use of idealized ages (e.g. 110 for the perfect Egyptian, 120 for the faithful Hebrew) had receded from use before the time of Christ.

- If you find that you are in disagreement with something you've been asked to learn, and you are writing (an assignment or exam), it may help to begin your answer with the words "Scholars say...." In this way, you are not committing yourself—especially if you need more time to process the material.

- Is the God of the Old Testament cruel? Highly recommended: Paul Copan, *Is God a Moral Monster?*

Religion (New Testament)
- It is important for Bible readers to know what happens in the centuries *not* covered by the Old and New Testaments. This means you need a basic understanding of intertestamental history. You also should read the Old Testament apocrypha. Note: The list of

apocryphal books in Roman Catholic Bibles is slightly different from that in Eastern Orthodox Bibles. And most protestant Bibles lack the apocrypha, although they were included in all Old Testaments from about 400 to 1700.

- Generally speaking, the letters are written before the gospels. However, there are elements in the New Testament that go back to the time of Jesus, found in the gospels or the epistles, and even in Acts. The oldest strata in the epistles are creedal statements and hymns, for example 1 Cor 15:3–4 and Php 2:6–11.

- Apart from most of the epistles and Revelation, the New Testament documents are anonymous. It does not matter very much who wrote them, although the evidence for the traditional authors does reach back to the second or third century. As with the Old Testament, it's the content of the New Testament that we understand is inspired, not any particular tradition about authorship.

- Radical scholars occasionally claim there's no proof Jesus even lived, apart from the Bible. This is false, and is disproved by a number of ancient Roman, Greek, Syrian, Jewish, and extrabiblical Christian sources.

- Some skeptics claim that Jesus' original words were lost. Actually, the process of oral tradition in ancient cultures was more than adequate to preserve the record of Jesus' words and deeds. Further, the Jews were renowned for their careful preservation of tradition, oral and written alike.

- However, in ancient *bios*, or biography, the rules are different from modern biography. Writers were allowed to put words in the mouth of characters, as long as those words accurately represented the person's view.

- Some scholars say that Jesus' divinity evolved. Actually, every section of the New Testament points to him as deity, from the earliest strata (early 30s) to the latest (in the 90s).

- Don't take your stand on the position that the manuscripts were error-free. First, it's not true. There are thousands of errors. Yet no doctrine of Christianity is affected by minor errors like misspellings or the odd missing word, especially with such a broad manuscript base. Historians seldom have access to such large numbers of ancient documents as Bible translators do.

- It is often said that Christ was a copy of other mythic figures, like Diogenes, Heracles, and Apollonius of Tyana. Yet the so-called parallels are too late, and the "parallels" are thin indeed.[63] Scholars put the final nail into this coffin over a century ago when the History of Religions School (a group of theologians connected to Germany's University of Gttingen in the late 1800s) roundly rejected this notion. Even so, this unsubstantiated allegation has been resurfacing of late.

- In Scripture, God uses accommodative language. He accommodates the message to our level of understanding, as though an adult were explaining something to a child. For example, when the Lord asks Adam, "Where are you?" it is not because God is ignorant. The question is for Adam's benefit—so that he will consider *where* he is spiritually. The Bible often speaks of the arm of the Lord—or his hand, wings, eyes, mouth, etc. Yet these images refer to the Lord's ability, strength, protection, omniscience, authority, and so forth. As in the incarnation, God comes down to our level. This point will prevent many misunderstandings.

Religion (World Religions)

- The word "tolerance" has undergone a substantial shift in meaning in recent decades, from acceptance of persons to acceptance of ideas. Many critics of Christianity are highly intolerant of Christians.

- We must help skeptics to understand that Christianity is *inclusive* (everyone is welcome), not exclusive (dividing people by status, race, nationality…). Everyone is welcome to the party!

- Yet all roads do *not* lead to God. They lead to vastly different destinies, whether the annihilation of Buddhism or the orgiastic paradise of Islam or the eternal fellowship with our loving Father.

- Western religions include three major faiths: Judaism, Christianity, and Islam. Eastern religions include two major faiths: Hinduism and Buddhism.

- All religions are definitely *not* the same; the differences greatly outweigh the similarities.

- In popular Buddhism there is the contradiction of reincarnation: the self has no true existence, so how can it be reincarnated?

- In classical Buddhism is the contradiction of self: nirvana comes when one realizes that he does not exist. Yet in this case, who is doing the desiring?
- In Hinduism, the soul ultimately becomes part of the world soul; all becomes one. In Buddhism, all is nothing. In neither case are relationships permanent. The end state is something impersonal.
- In Islam, Allah has ninety-nine names. None of those is Father. Nor do mainstream Muslims believe that God is love or that he loves sinners. Although Islam borrowed many features and doctrines of Judaism and Christianity, by this measure the Islamic god is not the God of the Bible.
- Islam has a number of scandalous doctrines, the suppression of women and jihad against infidels being the two most egregious.
- Violence is normative in Islam's Qur'an, and even more visible in the Hadith. Thus a Muslim waging war or doing violence follows his founder (Muhammad was a warrior), whereas a Christian practicing violence does so in spite of his master. Jesus practiced and taught nonviolence.
- Nearly 70% of the world is Muslim, Hindu, Buddhist, or (stated) atheist.[64] Since most of the world is not Christian—even nominally—we need to become familiar with worldviews if we're going to be able to engage.[65]

---

[50] Recommended: Francis Schaeffer, *How Should We Then Live?*

[51] On the day I wrote this section of the chapter, my wife and I attended an organ concert next door to the art museum of which we are members. The week before, we enjoyed the ballet (*The Nutcracker*). And in our home you will frequently hear the strains of a duet for piano and dog. (Our elder canine is quite the crooner, although "strains" is not an inappropriate word.) Despite these impressive facts, I am no artist, so if you are, or have further suggestions for the Arts sections that follow, please send an email. You can reach the author at drdajacoby@post.harvard.edu.

[52] A study of the issue of instrumental music may be found at http://www.douglas-jacoby.com/wp-content/uploads/2003/09/93Music.pdf.

[53] For me the study of Latin, once I took the challenge seriously, pulled me up from bottom of the class to the top (seventh grade). The discipline I learned through Latin transformed my study habits, and as a result I was able to graduate at the top of my high school class. Greek (a slightly more complex language) has also proved a great blessing, especially in being able to read the NewTestament without having

to rely on a lexicon.

[54] Highly recommended: Gordon Fee and Douglas Stuart, *How to Read the Bible for All Its Worth.*

[55] The modern perspective on morality and immorality separates private life from the public sphere. People naively imagine that one's private character shouldn't be taken into account when it comes to one's public life. Yet surely someone (like a CEO or politician) who has made thousands of little compromises is more likely, given something of importance to do (like run a company or a nation), to make a few big compromises. Further, a man who betrays his wife (adultery) may think little of selling out those who trust him to do what is right.

Next, modern society condones any behavior as long as it doesn't "hurt" others. At first this sounds somewhat reasonable. "Leave me alone—I'm not hurting anyone." But is this true? Moral choices affect everyone. Virtue has a leavening effect through society (Matt 5:13). Vice, like pollution, diminishes the quality of life for all. Further, while all sins are not equal, all sins are serious, from the "little ones" to "big sins." We may be horrified by murder, but what about premarital sex? How about slander or disrespect? All sin is a violation of God's will and is destructive.

- A person may think, "I'm not hurting anyone by throwing this trash on the ground." But is littering harmless? We all pay: collectively through higher taxes, or aesthetically by being forced to behold ugliness in place of natural beauty.
- Now consider gluttony. Are there any victims besides the gourmand? Yes—higher health premiums affect us all.
- All crimes, from tax evasion to bank robbery, drive up the cost of living, even if it wasn't *my* bank that was robbed.
- Indulging in porn assures the victimization of a steady stream of young women (and men and even children).
- Even if a drunk isn't driving, his poor judgment still affects others: absenteeism in effect lowers our wages (we have to work harder to cover for him); he probably hogs more than his fair share of health care, too.
- Gossip may seem trivial, but it unfairly affects how we view and interact with third parties.
- Academic cheating lowers educational standards and confirms the cheater in patterns that may well continue in the workplace.
- Materialism—the Bible calls it greed—feeds consumerism, which often furthers the exploitation of workers in the developing world.
- Sin twists our character, saps our moral strength (virtue) and integrity, and weakens our love for others. Sin affects the individual (guilt), but it also has social consequences, like alienation.
- When we act in violation of God's will, we sin against God. Of course in a godless world this wouldn't be the case—but then there'd be no morality, only preference. Since Christ died for us, we should never take sin lightly (Heb

10:26–31).

- Sin also affects others, even if it is committed in private. Sin diminishes our capacity to love. It erodes character. Like certain beverages and medications, it influences judgment—sooner or later somebody is going to be hurt (Gal 5:19–26).

[56] Recommended: Ravi Zacharias, *A Shattered Visage: The Real Face of Atheism and Can Man Live Without God?*

[57] In *Beyond Good and Evil* Nietzsche wrote: "There is no such thing as moral phenomena, but only a moral interpretation of phenomena," and also, "The whole of morality is a long, audacious falsification." No wonder he was Hitler's favorite philosopher. What Nietzsche meant was that the old world (God, absolutes, morality) is gone. We have undone it. If there's no God, then it's pointless to talk about right and wrong.

[58] God's existence may also be demonstrated through a simple syllogism, which constitutes powerful evidence for God's existence.

- If there's no universal good by which actions can be measured, then we may speak of preferences or opinions, but not of objective values.
- Objective morals do exist, and nearly anyone will concede the point.
- The conclusion follows directly from the premises: God exists.

[59] Is something good because God has commanded it, or has God commanded it because it is good? If the first, then good and evil are arbitrary; if the second, then good exists apart from God. Neither position is acceptable to a believer in the Judeo-Christian god.

[60] "[God] so regulates the knowledge of himself that he has given some signs of himself, visible to those who seek him and not to those who seek him not. There is enough obscurity for those who have a contrary disposition." —Blaise Pascal, *Pensées* 4.

[61] For a light survey of the whole Bible, see *A Quick Overview of the Bible.*

[62] Modern timekeeping has sexagesimal elements: 60 seconds in a minute, 60 minutes in an hour, and so on. For two helpful articles on the idealized ages, see http://www.douglasjacoby.com/q-a-1157-long-ages-of-genesis/.

[63] For example, it is said that Jesus' resurrection was nothing new. Yet the pagan divinities typically died and rose annually, whereas Jesus' death and resurrection were one-time events (Heb 9:25–28). Unlike the pagan gods, Jesus rose with a resurrection body, and not in the underworld, but on the earth. Another important difference: his resurrection was not tied to annual agricultural cycles, but to our perennial need for a Savior.

[64] There are currently 1.2 billion Roman Catholics, 800 million protestants, and nearly 300 million orthodox. World population in 2015 is approximately 7.3 billion.

[65] For a number of short podcasts on the various world religions, go to http://www.douglasjacoby.com/category/podcasts/various/world-religions/.

10. MATHEMATICS & PHYSICAL SCIENCES

After some prefatory comments about general science, we'll cover a number of subjects: astronomy, astrophysics, biology, biology (evolutionary), biology (exobiology), chemistry, environmental science, geology and earth science, mathematics, physics (general), physics (astrophysics), and physics (quantum mechanics).

Again, keep looking for biblical connections, arguments you may need to counter in the classroom, and occasional study tips.

Science (General)

- God speaks to us in various ways (Heb 1:1). The two main categories are general revelation and special revelation. Special revelation is *not* available to everyone; it is found in the history of ancient Israel, the person of Christ, and Scripture. General revelation is available to all the world, and comes through collective wisdom, conscience, and nature.

- God speaks through nature and Scripture. Science informs us about the world (nature), while the Bible brings us the Word (Scripture). This is the doctrine of the two books.[66]

- Natural law (the laws of science) implies a lawgiver.

- Science deals with the *how* of creation; Scripture addresses the *why*.

- A conflict between Bible and science means wrong theology or wrong science. Sometimes Bible interpreters err; sometimes scientists err.[67]

- Polytheistic religions do not lead to scientific discovery since there's no connection between a God of law and the laws of nature. Partial exception: Islam, which took up the mantle from Judaism and Christianity during the Middle Ages.

- Faith in the God of the Bible is the basis of modern science.[68]

- A large percentage of scientists believe in God—over 40% in the US alone.

- Phenomenological language should not be taken as unscientific. We all speak of sunrise and sunset.

- Dinosaurs are not mentioned in the Bible—nor are many other creatures and facts. They did not coexist with man, despite the oft-touted faked simultaneous tracks of humans and dinosaurs. Like ancient forests, the buried corpses of dinosaurs were transformed, under millennia of pressure, into fossil fuels.

- There are at least eight real things that lie beyond empirical verification: justice, love, beauty, number, God, logic, wisdom, and the soul.

- Insisting on empirical (scientific) proof when God is an immaterial being is itself illogical! Many things cannot be empirically proven, yet are real nonetheless.

- One cannot "prove" God through science—nor can anyone disprove him.

- Conservative Christians with a regard for science—including all science majors—should consider joining the American Scientific Affiliation. Contributors are Bible believers who seek to be faithful to both Scripture and nature.[69]

Astronomy and Astrophysics

- Scientists used to think the universe was infinite in two extents: time and space. Yet there is nothing beyond "empty space"; space itself has a boundary. And time has a beginning, probably 13.7 billion years ago.

- The Big Bang suggests creation and a Creator. According to the theory, nothing becomes something, then that something organizes into galactic and stellar and planetary systems, and in such a setting life is born. Not surprisingly, astrophysicists speak of the "creation."

- We ought to appreciate the enormity of the universe. If the initial explosion had been 1% weaker, the universe would long ago have collapsed on itself—no life. If the bang had been 1% stronger, the universe would continue to expand without the formation of stable star systems—big life. And given how many billions of years it takes for stars to convert hydrogen to helium and the heavier elements—disseminated throughout the galaxies by supernovas—the universe needed to be billions of years old before the key elements needed for life were present. All of this means that the universe, enormous as it is, *had* to be this size, in order for life to arise.

- Concerning the universe's coming into being, there are three possibilities.
  - ° The cosmos always existed. *Refuted by Big Bang cosmology.*
  - ° The cosmos created itself. *Not credible.*
  - ° The cosmos was created by an external power. *God is by far the likeliest explanation.*
- Bruno was burned at the stake for affirming that the earth revolves around the sun (1600). Galileo, following Copernicus, gave proof against heliocentrism and was placed under house arrest. It should be noted that many scriptures speak of a stationary, immovable, and flat earth. When the church took these passages to be teaching doctrine, she erred.
- Harvard astronomer Owen Gingrich says "The universe has been created with intention and purpose... this belief does not interfere with the scientific enterprise," and also "A common-sense and satisfying interpretation of our world suggests the designing hand of a superintelligence."
- The earth is placed in the optimal position for us to be able to study our galaxy and the universe. Nearer the center of the Milky Way, and light would interfere with our observational ability. Our moon also allows us to study the nearest star (the Sun) during solar eclipses. The sun and moon appear the same size in the sky because the diameter of the sun is about 400 times greater, while it is also 400 times farther away. If the moon were nearer *or* farther away from earth, we would not have the advantage in studying the sun's coronasphere—study yielding information about stars, the earth's origin, and relativity.
- For more material, see the "Physics" section.

Biology

- Just as mathematics is the universal "language" of physics, so DNA is the universal "language" of biology. DNA is information, code for the reproduction of cells. In this there is something complex yet simple, even elegant—a testimony to the work and wisdom of the Creator.

- God's creation was good, even "very good" (Gen 1:31)—although not necessarily perfect. Time and chance are part of the world order (Eccl 9:11). We ought not to blame God for permitting natural disasters, cancers, birth defects, and other causes of suffering in his universe. "Fearfully and wonderfully made" (Psalm 139:14) applies to the human race in general—how marvelous the human body is!—yet this applies even to those with birth defects.

- God's normal way of working is through processes. There are many, many examples: childbirth, forestation, photosynthesis, nuclear fission in stars, etc. He is not in a rush—eons of time are not an issue.

- Nor does God micromanage. This explains the propagation of coding errors during DNA replication, natural disasters, and more.

- See further comments under "Medicine."

Biology (Evolutionary)

- The Book of Genesis is not, and was not intended to be, a science or history book. It was written to demonstrate that God accomplishes his work in an orderly fashion, not through unbridled chaos. Genesis also critiques the idolatrous systems of Israel's neighbors. Ultimately the Bible is a book about the "why" of creation, while science continues to struggle to explain the how, and history tries to concur/verify scientific conclusions.

- Read the *Origin of Species*, or at least a credible synopsis (one without an agenda). It's not appropriate to have strong (often negative) opinions and feelings about Darwin if we've never taken the trouble to read his books or letters.[70]

- Beware of specious arguments—some of which are spread in church. For example, "If evolution is true, then we're only animals! *Your* great-great-great-grandfather may have been an ape; *mine* wasn't." The Bible classifies us as both *belonging to* and *ruling over* the animals—but only when we live spiritually, faithfully bearing the image of God. Otherwise, we descend to the level of the flesh. Genetically we have much in common with other animals. Yet, unlike them, we have a choice: to live by the flesh or to live by the Spirit![71]

- You may also have heard, "Evolution is only a theory, not fact." I used to say this myself! But that's not how the word *theory* is used in science. A theory is a comprehensive explanation of the facts, a way of making sense of the data. Gravitation is a theory, yet that hardly means we would be safe skydiving without a parachute. Einstein forever changed how gravity is understood, but he didn't render gravity obsolete. At any rate, evolution is well supported by facts: the fossil record, speciation in progress today, and the findings of genetics. It is possible that a better theory, or a different version of the theory, will one day undermine our current understanding.[72] Evolution isn't sacrosanct, just the best model for what is observed.

- Many other specious claims made about evolutionary biology[73] have, unfortunately, set up young believers to fail spiritually. Once they take college level biology, they're confronted with the evidence. They realize that much of what they heard in church, though well intended, was not based on the facts. If you have been told you have to choose between science and faith, remember that God speaks in *two* books, the Bible and his creation (Rom 1:20; Psalm 19; 104). You *don't* have to choose.

- Fortunately, our salvation does not depend on our understanding of any scientific position. There are, in fact, five basic positions on the origin of life. Christians hold to the second, third, and fourth position. The position of virtually all Christians in science is Evolutionary Creation.

  ○ *Deistic creationism* – Enlightenment (many Founding Fathers of the US). This position denies miracles, answered prayer, the incarnation, etc. God set up the world and left it to operate on its own, like a clock.

  ○ *Old earth creationism* – Discovery Institute (High Ross). This camp, accepting the longevity of the earth proved by science, typically views the creation days of Genesis 1 as eons of time. Evolution is accepted on the whole, although God is necessary for the really big jumps (e.g. among orders or phyla).

○   *Young earth creationism* – Answers in Genesis (Ken Ham). Takes the creation days literally, relying on the genealogies to approximate the date of creation. Accept minor biological development (microevolution), but not macroevolution.

○   *Evolutionary creation* – Biologos (Francis Collins). Also called theistic evolution. Holds that God accomplished his purposes through evolution, and accepts evolutionary biology.

○   *Atheistic evolution* – Atheist Alliance International (Richard Dawkins). The forces that led to life are impersonal. Nor is there a meaning to the cosmos, apart from the one we assign to it.

Exobiology (Extraterrestrial Life)

- Extraterrestrial life forms have not yet been detected, though their existence is appearing increasingly likely.

- That ET is not mentioned in the Bible is unremarkable. Neither does the Bible mention uranium, pterodactyls, or the planet Uranus. Unless ET served an important purpose for humankind, there would be little point in mentioning it in Scripture.

- Note: The "UFOs" described in Ezekiel 1 are nothing of the kind.

- Even if ET does exist, this would pose no problem biblically. If these beings are intelligent and moral—two assumptions—*and* fallen, they are reconciled through Christ (Eph 3:15; Col 1:16), and if not, then they have no need for a Savior in the first place.

- The laws of chemistry restrict the possibilities for extraterrestrials. There are only two elements in the universe suitable for large (as opposed to microbial) animals, and they are Si and C. An animal whose body chemistry was based on Si would tend to be small and flat—scarcely three-dimensional. C is the element with bonding sites best suited for three-dimensional animal life. Thus organic chemistry would be the same throughout the cosmos; advanced life forms would roughly approximate our own body forms.

- The bond-angles of hydrogen atoms with oxygen make possible H_2O that freezes from the top down; is a universal solvent; and comprises the majority of most life forms.

Chemistry

- Consider the simplicity amidst complexity of the Periodic Table. All matter is made out of the 92 elements in the Periodic Table (plus a few very heavy elements that exist for only a fraction of a second).
- The early universe was abundant in hydrogen, though through nuclear fusion more and more helium was formed. Eventually atoms of carbon, nitrogen, and oxygen came into existence. The cores of stars are furnace-factories where heavier and heavier elements are built up.
- The "laws" of chemistry suggest order, logic, wisdom—and a Creator.

Environmental Science

- Concern for the creation appears on page 1 of your Bible. God tasks humans to exercise dominion over the creation (Gen 1:28).
- How do humans relate to nature? Where do we as humans fit into the scheme of things? Genesis 1 and 2 (esp. 1:26–27; 2:7) indicate our natural origins ("day six" creation along with the other beasts, made from dirt). Yet there is also a divine origin, and humans are tasked with bearing (or being) the divine image. (This is not "speciesism.") We are in *both* worlds. We should be *honored* to be God's children, yet *humbled* by our earthly origins.
- What duties, or obligations, if any, do humans have towards the natural world? According to Genesis 1:26 and 28; Genesis 2:15; Psalm 8:6; and many other passages, and in line with extensive Judeo-Christian reflection on passages such as Luke 16:12 and 19:17 and 1 Corinthians 4:2, we have a responsibility to care for the creation. That is, ecology is part of spirituality. One clear example of ecological responsibility is the Sabbath principle in agriculture (Exo 23:10–11; Lev 26:34–35; 2 Chr 36:21).
- As ultraconservative Christians generally oppose the evidence for global warming, you will break the stereotype—I think that's a good thing—by letting it be known that you hold the conclusions of the scientific community in high regard, even if on some issues

you say, "The jury's still out."

- What about the Green Movement? This does not work if there is no God, or if, as many New Age thinkers opine, we are only part of nature. For in that case what argument, on the basis of naturalism, could be made that we shouldn't trash the planet, kill the weak, commit adultery, and so forth? With biblical monotheism there is a warrant for ecology. Either we are only part of nature (like the other animals, and thus without moral responsibility), or we somehow transcend nature, as Scripture teaches, and thus are responsible for our ethics—environmental, familial, business, sexual, social, etc. Thus the Green Movement falls short, for it fails to achieve the insight that this is God's world. (Psalm 104 powerfully attests to this fact.) So ask your "green" friends why ecology matters if there's no God. It really goes back to the moral issue; in a godless world nothing is right or wrong. (See "Philosophy [Ethics].") Explain why ecology follows naturally from the mandate of Genesis 1.

Geology and Earth Science

- Stars disseminate metals throughout the cosmos; volcanism brings metals to the surface; all this makes technology possible.[74]
- The metal in the core of the earth saves our lives. By its generating the earth's magnetic field, cosmic radiation, which otherwise would fry us, is bounced away.
- When land first appeared, there was but one supercontinent. Pangaea and plate tectonics are for real; don't doubt them.
- The geological column had been sorted out by 1800—by Bible believers—implying a world at least hundreds of thousands, if not millions, of years old.
- Flood geology, popularized by Morris and Whitcomb in 1961,[75] fails to account for the fossils in the geological column.
    - Extinct groups are found in most levels up to the geological present day. This would not be the case if these animals had been on the Ark.
    - A flood would not gently sort out carcasses of animals, as well as plants, in the same order worldwide. Rather, every-

thing would be mixed together.

    o There *is* evidence of flooding worldwide—yet not for a single flood. Instead, numerous local floods, thousands and millions of years apart, have affected the planet.

    o Some of the flood narratives are based on missionary re-telling of Noah's Flood. Yet flooding is so common in our world that it would be surprising if communities forgot these and other cataclysms.

- There is abundant evidence for an ancient earth.[76] For measuring extreme ages, radiometric dating is the most reliable method. Some "Young Earthers" suggest that, under different conditions, decay rates may have been faster in the past, thus leading us to think the world is older than it is. Yet scientists have experimented with varying the conditions (temperature, pressure, and so on); there is zero evidence that decay rates are affected by altered conditions.

- Christians have a deep regard for the earth. According to one school of thought, we will not be taken "up" to heaven. Rather, heaven comes "down" to us. If this is correct, then earth will be our eternal home.[77] Either way, the Lord has charged us to take care of the planet.

Mathematics

- Mathematics is the universal language of physics, just as DNA is the language of biology. Mathematics transcends all earthly languages.

- There is evidence of mathematical elegance in the physical world.

    o Number theory has its own beauty.

    o Consider the amazing numbers π, e, Φ.[78]

    o Consider the Fibonacci series, fractals, etc.

- Numbers are real—yet without being physical things. Much of reality is nonphysical; see the discussion under "Science (General)."

- The world of mathematics suggests there is a God.[79]

Physics

- Physics deals with *physis,* nature, not supernature. Just because physics doesn't help understanding what is *beyond* physics (origin word, *meta*physical) doesn't mean there isn't anything beyond nature. Reminder: Science is limited in its reach.
- Physical laws are written in the language of mathematics; without the regularity of scientific law, or without the tools mathematics provides, we would be able to understand very little of our world.
- Physical laws imply a lawgiver.
- The universal language of physics is mathematics. In this we see the hand of God—elegant, logical, orderly, trustworthy.

Quantum Mechanics

- Heisenberg's Uncertainty Principle does *not* suggest that everything is relative, or that there are no absolutes. (In that case, the principle would be self-refuting.)
- The Higgs Boson is the much-celebrated "God particle," as detected in 2012. Yet even if the four fundamental forces are fully understood (electricity-magnetism, gravity, the strong nuclear force, and the weak nuclear force), this would not rule out God.
- If you take classes in this area, remember, "Truth is often stranger than fiction," and also "Whoever claims he understands [quantum physics], doesn't."[80]
- The "multiverse" is a theoretical notion only. There is no evidence, it's purely speculative, and even if this speculation is correct, this only pushes back the question of where it all came from. We would still be left looking for a Creator.
- If some scientists are going to posit a multiverse in order to explain the world as it is, it's hard to see why Christians should be criticized for proposing that God is the cause. Neither can be proved scientifically. Yet the hypothesis of God has far greater explanatory power.

---

[66] A great quote I have found useful in apologetics presentations is "Let no man or woman, out of conceit or laziness, think or believe that anyone can search too far or be too well informed in the Book of God's Words or in the Book of God's Works:

Religion or Science. Instead, let everyone endlessly improve their understanding of both."—Francis Bacon, 1605.

[67] Highly recommended: Thomas S. Kuhn, *The Structure of Scientific Revolutions.*

[68] The following were all Bible believers as well as important contributors to science: Agassiz—ichthyology, Babbage—computers, Boyle—chemistry, Faraday—magnetism, Kelvin—thermodynamics, Kepler—astronomy, Lister—antiseptic surgery, Maxwell—electrodynamics, Mendel—genetics, Newton—physics, Pascal—hydrostatics, Pasteur—bacteriology, Ramsay—isotropic chemistry, Simpson—gynecology, Steno—stratigraphy.

[69] The website of the American Scientific Affiliation is www.asa3.org. Note: You don't have to be American to join.

[70] Darwin is often called an atheist, whereas agnostic is the more accurate term. Interestingly, his wife was a Bible believer, and Darwin continued to donate to support world missions until his dying day. Further, when Darwin released his *The Origin of Species* (1859), some of his biggest fans were Bible believers. For a list of helpful titles, please go to www.douglasjacoby.com and click on Books & More > Recommended > Creation & Evolution. For a short video presentation, watch *Science & Faith: Enemies or Allies?*

[71] For those insulted by the notion of human evolution, it gets worse. The Bible describes us as made of earth (Gen 2:7). Dirt! *Adam,* which is a play on words with *'adamah* (the word for earth, ground, dust), reminds us of our lowly origins and our heavenly Creator. Remembering our origins should keep us humble!

[72] The claim "Scientists disagree over evolution" is misleading. Few theories in the history of science have won as wide a following. Of course biologists don't all agree with one another on everything, even about some aspects of evolution. But it's misleading to take this to mean that they reject the theory. It is true that some scientists outside the field of biology qualify their acceptance of evolution, but for those who work in such areas as genetics, molecular biology, botany, and zoology, the theory is a given. More than ninety-nine percent of scientists accept it. This is not to say that most scientists look to the theory for meaning; the majority of scientists in our world are believers, standing in awe of God's ways, and are usually careful about worshiping only the Creator, not his creation.

[73] There is much misinformation about evolution.

- The claim "Scientists unfairly rule out the supernatural" is questionable. Science deals with nature, not supernature; it's neither for nor against the supernatural. A Geiger counter has no bias against kilograms; it just can't weigh them. Neither is science prejudiced against symphonies. It has nothing to say about musical beauty, even if it can explain the acoustics of sound. A few scientists do have an antifaith agenda, and trade on their authority in one (fairly small) domain to lecture others on faith—though in my experience most scientists are persons of integrity.

- Some preachers teach that fiat creation must be instantaneous. Their reasoning goes something like this: *"Bara'* is Hebrew for *ex nihilo* (out of nothing) creation, in contrast with *'asah,* meaning to shape (to make or form from preexisting material), and *bara',* not *'asah,* is used in Genesis 1." This argument doesn't work. First, Genesis uses *bara'* in both senses, and the words are nearly synonyms. *Bara'* is the verb used in Isaiah 44:21, where God speaks of having created Israel. Yet she came to be a people through a process spanning centuries, with many twists and turns along the way. The notion that it is beneath God to act slowly is flawed.

- Genesis 1 contains one of five or six creation stories in the Bible. In Gen 1, creation is portrayed as taking place in a week, probably to emphasize the importance of Sabbath for the Jews. This account is semipoetic. Historically speaking, most Jews and Christians during the last two or three millennia have not taken this literally. There are more ways of reading the days of Genesis 1 than just the literal interpretation.

- Some claim that we can't trust the fossil evidence, since sometimes things are backwards, or the expected geological strata are missing. In fact, the sequences are invariable, although occasionally layers are destroyed by erosion (e.g. with the land heaving and subsiding, to be exposed to water) or overturned through colossal natural forces (like volcanic eruption).

- Others object, "Mutations are harmful, and could never lead to any significant improvement—much less to the development of new structures or species." Yet the harmful mutations are weeded out as the life forms affected by them lose out in the struggle to pass on genes. The accumulation of mutations that bring a survival advantage leads to new structures and species. New species are continually developing on the planet. *Scientific American, Nature,* and other journals can guide us through the latest discoveries.

- Still more claim, "The earth is only a few thousand years old, far too young for evolution to have happened." Yet there are dozens of accurate dating techniques, and all suggest a world enormously older than any estimate the Young Earth Movement has ever suggested. On the other hand, unless God had set the initial conditions ("fine-tuning for life"), the chance of our world coming into existence would have been infinitesimal. If the atheists are right, the world is way too young to have gotten so lucky.

- "Evolution violates the Second Law of Thermodynamics." This law, regarding thermodynamic systems, holds that total entropy (the tendency of a system to move to disorganization) is conserved, or even increases. While this is true for a closed system, the earth is not a closed system. It continuously receives inputs of energy (like sunlight) and mass (like meteors), which feed and drive a number of processes (like photosynthesis).

- "Hitler appealed to evolution to justify his inhuman actions." The Crusaders appealed to the Bible, too, but their erroneous applications don't nullify Scripture. Nazism was (and is) horrible, and no doubt its engineers misused science to further their ends. However, even though the objection carries a lot of emotional freight, it isn't relevant to the discussion of whether evolution is true.

• "Evolution is a slippery slope." Some fear that if they accept evolution, they're opening the door to atheism. This need not be so. Consider the literature of the Bible. Roughly one third of Scripture is poetic. Does acknowledging the poetry somehow lead to rejecting the historical facts of the Bible? Can't people tell the difference? The earth is described as resting atop pillars (Job 9:6; 26:11; Ps 75:3), yet surely this is the ancient concept, incidental and not a matter of doctrine. Does accepting a spherical earth lead to total rejection of the Bible? The slope becomes slippery only when faith is incorrectly linked with the rejection of a neutral theory (evolution). Without distinguishing ancient conceptions from modern science, we end up in a tangle.

74 See Michael Denton's classic, *Nature's Destiny*. Although Denton is an old earth creationist, his arguments in *Nature's Destiny* are unassailable. (When I first read it, I bought ten copies for friends!)

75 Their influential book was *The Genesis Flood*. For a balanced and Christian examination of these claims in the light of geology, read Davis Young, *The Biblical Flood*.

76 See Alan Hayward, *Creation and Evolution*. Darrel R. Falks's *Coming to Peace with Science: Bridging the World Between Faith and Biology* is also very good.

77 Although I am not persuaded by this view, I did devote a chapter to it in my book *What's the Truth about Heaven and Hell?*

78 For non-mathematicians, π is the quotient of the circumference of a circle divided by twice its radius; e is the base of natural logarithms; and Φ is the golden mean, when a geometric shape's dimensional ratio is (a+b)/a = a/b. All three of these special numbers are irrational, with approximate values of 3.1415926536, 2.7182818285, and 1.6180339887, respectively.

79 See https://www.quora.com/What-are-the-mathematical-proofs-of-Gods-existence.

80 Recommended: Robert Gilmore, *Alice in Quantumland: An Allegory of Quantum Physics,* http://www.amazon.com/Alice-Quantumland-Allegory-Quantum-Physics/dp/0387914951.

11. PROFESSIONAL STUDIES

In this final chapter we'll comment on eight professional courses: business studies, computer science, criminology, education, engineering, law, medicine, and social work. (Several of these could just as easily be categorized under different headings.)

Business Studies

- *Integrity:* the corporate world has a strong culture of corruption and deceit. Many younger professionals believe the only way they can advance their careers is by taking shortcuts, vilifying coworkers, and conniving their way to the top. The Bible provides several examples of individuals who worked hard and gained more responsibility (a.k.a. promotions) because of their integrity and relationship with God (think Joseph, Daniel). See also the comments on "Integrity" in Chapter 4.

- *Conviction:* the corporate world often contains a strong "work hard, play hard" type culture where long hours are expected, along with heavy networking usually accompanied by intense drinking. This type of lifestyle is often expected, encouraged, and praised in order to advance your career and social status within your firm. Christians are expected to work hard, but be more known for their conviction and love rather than their willingness to grab beers with coworkers after work. There are lots of biblical examples to support how Christians should maintain conviction in their workspace (Daniel again, Esther, Nehemiah). Our conviction can be the most powerful tool for turning the hearts and minds of coworkers.

- *Selfishness:* the corporate world is a selfish place. Due to the high incomes and egos, much time is spent building oneself up and building a life filled with material possessions and experiences. This usually creates intense loneliness and a severe lack of depth in the direction of one's life. As Christians, we have great answers to these problems: Jesus Christ, a church community, a clear and meaningful direction, a desire to serve and lift others up, etc. These are good things to keep in mind when trying to connect and build relationships with coworkers. Always remember that the majority of coworkers are looking for answers to their selfishness and loneliness. Jesus has the answers.

- The world of business and finance speaks of "net worth," calculated by subtracting liabilities from assets. Yet our true value isn't financial, or physical (the going rate for our organs), or even how much others think of us. We are precious to our God, who knows our true worth.

- Money has an intoxicating quality. If your goal is to make all the money you can so that you can give away as much as you can, you are unusual. I knew a brother who, while he was single, gave 50% of his salary back to the church and the needy. We need more people like Zacchaeus (Luke 19:1–10).

- In the world people use people and love things—instead of loving people and using things. We must resist the world's messages—many of which are relayed through advertising—which are inimical to loving our neighbor.

- Occasionally your boss might ask you to "break the rules." As persons of integrity, we must find a way to refuse.[81]

- If we are in marketing, we shouldn't need the government to enforce truth in advertising. We represent the service or product honestly and with integrity, because of the One whom we follow. Ask: Am I influencing people to buy things they don't need, especially if this will push them into debt? We may not be our brother's keeper, but we are to follow the Golden Rule (Matt 7:12).

- Business should enhance social justice. Corrupt business practices are addressed in many books of the Bible (the Torah, Amos, and James, for example).

- It is part of biblical ethics to consider supply chains. For example, one prophet criticized those who sold the needy for a pair of sandals (Amos 2:6; 8:6).

- One reason the Lord gave us the Sabbath was so that work would not take over our lives. We should resist the urge to produce seven days a week (Neh 13:19–22).

- See also the points under "Economics."

Computer Science/Information Technology

- Computer prowess can foster illusions of omniscience and control. Stay humble.

- Artificial intelligence is truly amazing, and no doubt computers will continue to evolve and impress, mimicking life. Yet machines lack consciousness, conscience, self-awareness, and more. We must never forget the difference between tool and toolmaker.

- Communication is a divine activity. Information has existed all along. "In the beginning was the Word" (John 1:1). Since the Lord is a communicating God, we too take communication seriously.

- The worldwide web is a wonderful tool—yet it has a dark side. We must honor Christ as we navigate the web.

- There's a delicate balance between technology as servant and technology as master. Technology tends to encroach on all areas of our lives. Jesus might have said, "Technology was made for man, not man for technology" (in the spirit of Mark 2:27).

- It is easy to be drawn into the artificial world of computers and cyberspace, making interacting with computers a substitute for human interaction. Give careful consideration to what kind of company you will work for; if tight deadlines are the norm, they may expect you to make your job your life.

Criminology

- Is crime really sickness, instead of sin? To what extent may crime be a cause *and* an effect? This is an important question to ponder and a hot topic among jurists and psychiatrists alike.

- God is a god of justice, and so ultimately all crime is against God (Ps 51:4).

- The principle of deterrence—see Eccl 8:11.

- Oppression, injustice, systemic corruption—see Eccl 5:8–9.

- Convicting the guilty—see Proverbs 24:25. There will be a day of reckoning, and it will be fair.[82] Though it may take a while, it will certainly come (Hab 1:2–2:3; Num 32:23; 1 Tim 5:24).

- No one is above the law. In the Old Testament the same laws applied to king as applied to commoner. This was highly unusual in the ancient world. It is still rare in the modern world.

- The prophets spoke out against social injustice (Elijah, Micah, Amos, John the Baptist, and many others). Jesus challenged leaders of his day, reminding high priest, governor, and other authorities of important spiritual principles they had ignored. There are times when believers must speak up—speak out!

- The State has the right to impose penalties: fines, traffic tickets; imprisonment; execution (Rom 13:4).

- Incarceration in ancient times was temporary, for example for those awaiting trial. Long-term imprisonment was more likely for kings' enemies or those of whom rulers did not want to make martyrs. Paul (Acts 24, 28) and Joseph (Gen 39–41) are unusual in the length of their incarcerations.

- Prisoners were visited by friends or relatives—fed, clothed, and cared for by them. The state did little (see Jeremiah 37–38).

- Does our system of incarceration work? To what extent is it "correctional," or "penitentiary"? Is there "reformation" of character, or recidivism? What if crime were personalized, as follows: if criminals (ID theft, burglary, murder) had to face those they victimized, or their families, maybe there could be true change at a heart level. The system works poorly, though in some nations the penal system is more effective than in others.[83]

- Capital punishment, although specified for nearly twenty Old Testament crimes,[84] was in most cases commuted to a financial penalty (Num 35:31–32). The situation changed under the New Covenant. The early Christians were aware of capital punishment (Rom 13:4).[85] The early church rejected capital punishment.[86]

- Prison ministry? In New Testament times, prisoners would normally have been believers (Heb 10:34; 13:23). And yet prisons present a great evangelistic opportunity. Consider the implications of Philippians 1:7 1:12–14, and 4:22.

- See also the pointers under "Law."

Education

- Education is an appropriate career for those who follow *the* Teacher (Matt 23:8).

- A great teacher can make almost any subject interesting!

- Those who teach should do so with an attitude of sobriety and humility (James 3:1; Luke 6:39–40). They should desire to be teachers for love of teaching, not because they will have summers off and spring breaks!

- In the Middle Ages, university students studied the liberal arts.[87] This course assumed one would be active in the public sphere. Education was for engagement, communication, and understanding of the world—for the good of society. The modern move to one narrow discipline means even holders of multiple degrees may lack the big picture when it comes to understanding the physical world, human civilization, the meaning of life, etc.

- Squeezing God out of educational institutions is intellectually dishonest, as religion has lain at the core of civilization for countless centuries, and has in most cases supplied the impetus for learning in the first place!

- And (for later, after you qualify): teachers have a basic level of training but then many, if not most, fail to continue to grow intellectually and in character.

- Be aware of anti-Christian bias in the media and within the academy. What would happen if a kid brought a Bible to show-and-tell? A Qur'an?

- Pick your battles carefully, especially if you are working in a secular country like the United States, where any hint of religion can lead to the teacher being disciplined or even defrocked.

- Education is hardly the enemy of faith, but its servant. The Lord wants us to use our minds. The Torah says we are to love the Lord with all our heart, soul, and strength (Deut 6:5). Jesus adds a word: *mind* (Matt 22:37; Mark 12:30; Luke 10:27), emphasizing the need to think.

Engineering

- Unless the Lord builds the house, the builders labor in vain (Ps 127:1).

- The Old Testament has at least one massive building project: the temple. Only by detailed plans, delegation of tasks (to workers empowered and gifted by God to accomplish certain tasks), and trustworthy oversight is such a project realistic. Blueprints are biblical.

- Engineering requires mathematical rigor, patience, and attention to minute detail. Think of Moses carefully following the plans for the construction of the tabernacle (Exod 25:9).

- If we are engineers or math students, we can easily end up with minds so analytical that we lose sensitivity to beauty, or fail in relationships. Strive to develop your artistic side.[88]

- Our ultimate hope is for a divinely engineered home, a "city with foundations" (Heb 11:10; Rev 21:19–20).

Law

- Much of modern law derives from the ancient Romans. More comes from the legal system and case law of the Old Testament, like property law, torts, worker's compensation, litigation, etc. (Exod 20–Deut 33).

- There is a huge difference of emphasis between the Law of Hammurabi and the Torah. The Babylonians seemed most concerned with property crimes; people were less valuable. Keep this in mind in an arena where one may receive a stricter sentence for plucking a protected plant than for armed robbery!

- In OT law we perceive God's wisdom, providence, and justice. Even though it isn't the *law* of God for us, it is still the *word* of God for us, and we have much to learn!

- Not everything that's legal is ethical. Smoking pot may be legalized; adultery has long been legal in most nations; profanity and pornography are permitted, with few restrictions. Yet God's people don't look to lawmakers and judges to tell us what's moral or ethical. For that we have God and his word.

- It will go well with those who convict the guilty (Prov 17:15; 24:24–25). If you're only helping the guilty or the powerful take advantage of the weak and the poor, you're in sin.

- At the same time God approves of measures to safeguard the innocent, especially when in the heat of the moment justice may not be meted out. Consider the cities of refuge (Num 35:6).

- The *Lex talionis* (law of retribution, or "an eye for an eye") was just, strictly speaking (Exo 21:24). Yet its goal wasn't "payback" for the one wronged, but limiting the punishment. The human tendency is to demand a pound of flesh—and more (Gen 4:24). Of course Jesus went further. While in the Old Testament the punishment had to fit the crime, Jesus asked that we not seek to get even (Matt 18:21–22); this passage is a direct allusion to the vengeance of Lamech.

- Law, for a Christian, ought not to be about the salary, but about standing up for truth. The law doesn't require lawyers to have posh lifestyles.[89] Consider carefully whether your lifestyle is pleasing to the Lord.

- There are several professions that can take your soul. God and other relationships are squeezed out of your schedule; people take themselves too seriously (believing their own press). At special risk: lawyers, doctors, business executives, ministers.

- In the practice of law, you may be expected to compromise the truth or blatantly lie. What is the character of the attorneys for whom you work? Is it about winning at any cost?

- Be careful about working late at night, especially when in close contact with the opposite sex. Similarly, business travel can be an occasion for sin. The need for honesty and accountability is great.

- See further pointers under "Criminology."

Medicine

- Jesus is *the* Great Physician (Luke 4:23; Mark 2:17; Jer 8:22). On earth he was known not only for his competence, but also for his compassion. Patients appreciate kindness, empathy, and patience—the personal touch. Not every physician has this, so begin working on your "bedside manner" in med school. Will your priority be the number of patients you can see in a day to maximize billings, or more appropriate scheduling to have the time needed to listen to, comfort, and heal your patients?

- Medical care can be expensive—and it doesn't always work (Mark 5:26). Yet even when the Great Physician was on this earth, not all were healed. Apparently, immediate healing was not God's will in the majority of cases. Healthy or not, "thorn" or no "thorn" (2 Cor 12:7; 1 Tim 5:23; 2 Tim 4:20), we are to look to the Lord for our well-being.

- Consider the irony of the Hippocratic Oath, once honored by doctors. Even in an era when life was cheap, Hippocrates (c.460–c.370 BC) forbade abortion, infanticide, and euthanasia. The oath also prohibits charging for medical training and becoming amorously involved with patients. Medical schools today use a truncated (and more lucrative) version of the oath.

- On the issue of abortion, beware of taking an unnecessarily polarized position. Our stance as Christians will depend on how we interpret certain verses, like Exo 21:22–23, and whether or not we believe the fertilized zygote becomes fully human on a continuum or at a discrete time.[90] While holding to biblical conviction uncompromisingly, still we need to behave and speak with genuine concern for others.

- Consider the vanity of plastic surgery. This seems wholly legitimate in the case of injury, wound, or birth defect, but to attract the opposite sex? And isn't it sinful to value looking physically better than your neighbors, at least according to current cultural preferences, rather than pursuing inner beauty? (Exod 20:17; Prov 31:30; 1 Pet 3:3–4).

- Although prayer may contribute towards healing (James 5:13–16), healing normally occurs through the practice of medicine. Yet we are not to put our faith *exclusively* in medicine (2 Chr 16:12).

- The pressure of medical school and working as a physician are considerable. You need someone who can keep you accountable, so that you excel as a Christian before you excel in medicine.

Social Work

- Social workers take seriously the importance of ministering to the *whole* person—a core biblical emphasis (1 Thess 5:23; 3 John 2). The Hebrew concept of *shalôm*,[91] which is wholeness or peace, is the goal of such service.

- Most of those engaged in social work are compassionate, patient, and genuinely interested in others' welfare. Would that all God's people were the same!

- In the earliest Christian centuries, "brothers" in Matthew 25:31–46 were interpreted as brothers in Christ, not outsiders. This was not a refusal to help unbelievers, but rather a priority of helping fellow Christians (Gal 6:10). Moreover, the Good Samaritan (Luke 10:25–37) reached out to a needy person *outside* his people, so it would be wrong to create a Christian enclave in which believers hide from the world. Another consideration is that the Old Testament repeatedly charges God's people to care for the alien, along with the widow and the orphan (Exo 22:21–24; Psalm 146:9). If this is so, two things follow. First, the church needs to be involved in social work, starting at home. Second, we need to be alert to the needs of outsiders all around us. True justice or righteousness means extending God's *shalom* to the world.

- Don't look down on fellow Christians whose ministries don't resemble your own. Be willing to wrap yourself with the towel and get to work (John 13:4–5, 15–17). And don't become puffed up because you're such a servant—the ultimate irony.

---

[81] See the helpful article in the *Harvard Business Review,* 7 January 2016, by Peter T. Coleman and Robert Ferguson: https://hbr.org/2016/01/what-to-do-if-your-boss-asks-you-to-break-the-rules.

[82] Genesis 18:25; Luke 12:47-48; Romans 2:5; 14:10; 2 Corinthians 5:10; Hebrews 9:27; 2 Peter 3:7; 1 John 4:17; etc.

[83] The US, with 5% of the world's population, holds some 25% of the world's prisoners. China, with a less glorious human rights record, has far fewer behind bars.

[84] The Old Testament has capital punishment for adultery (Lev 20:10); attacking parents (Exod 21:15); bestiality (Exod 22:19; Lev 20:15); blasphemy (Lev 24:16); bull goring (Exod 21:29); contempt of court (Deut 17:12); cursing parents (Exod 21:17; Lev 20:9); female promiscuity (Deut 22:21); hoodlum children (Deut 21:18–21); idolatry (Exod 22:20; Deut 13:5; 17:2–5); incest (Lev 20:11–12); kidnapping (Exod 21:16; Deut 24:7); malicious witness in a capital case (Deut 19:16–19); manslaughter (Gen 9:6; Exod 21:12; Lev 24:17; Num 35:16ff); priestly arrogation (Num 3:10; 18:7); Sabbath breaking (Num 15:35); sodomy (Lev 20:13); and sorcery (Exod 22:18; Lev 20:27).

[85] The sword (decapitation) was for Roman citizens, though it is unlikely that James (Acts 12:2) and John the Baptist (Mark 6:27) were citizens. Beheading is also evident

in the martyrs of the Apocalypse (Rev 20:4). Slaves and the vilest criminals might be crucified. Recommended: Martin Hengel, *The Cross of the Son of God.*

[86] "When they know that we cannot endure even to see a man put to death, though justly, who of them can accuse us of murder?... We consider that to see a man put to death is much the same as killing him… So how can we put people to death?" —Athenagoras (c. AD 175), 2.147. Also Origen (c. AD 248), 4.6; Cyprian (c. AD 250), 5.351; Lactantius (c. AD 304–313), 7.186–187. References are in *Ante-Nicene Fathers,* by the standard volume and page numbers.

[87] In the Middle Ages universities offered instruction in the seven liberal arts. The *quadrivium* consisted of arithmetic, geometry, music, and astronomy; the *trivium* consisted of grammar, rhetoric, and logic. The aim was not only to know the truth about how the world worked, but to become clear thinking and persuasive in interactions with others.

[88] Recommended: *How to Think like Leonardo Da Vinci: Seven Steps to Genius Every Day,* by Michael J. Gelb.

[89] I have a friend who was able to support his family by working one day a week in practicing law—devoting the remaining time to his personal ministry.

[90] For a broad study of the issues involved, see http://www.douglasjacoby.com/abortmp3/.

[91] *Shalôm* is picked up by the apostle Paul in his greetings. In the east, people wished one another "peace." Jews said *"Shalom"* and the Arabs *"Salaam."* In the west (the Greek-speaking world of the Roman Empire) a standard opening for an epistle was "Greetings" (Greek *chairein,* as in Acts 15:23). Paul, the apostle who preached the gospel to Jew and Gentile alike, combines the terms, as in Philippians 1:2. "Grace," *charis,* is similar to the word *chairein.* Thus in Christ we acknowledge the "grace and peace" of the Lord. The greeting itself is an emblem of unity.

IV. FOLLOW-THROUGH

Campus ministry is dynamic—there isn't time to dwell on past victories when growth is consistently on the horizon. A mindset of merely "holding down the fort" is a recipe for failure, since every year students graduate into the working world and must be "replaced" if the ministry isn't going to shrink. Wise campus leaders maintain momentum while keeping the ministry healthy and well anchored. How can this lofty goal be reached? Our first chapter in Section IV, "Crucial Counsel for Campus Ministers," will probably be of interest to all members of your campus group.

Next, we will consider an array of options past graduation. Some graduates will continue their formal education as they pursue masters or doctorate degrees; some will not. Does grad school make financial sense? How should this decision be made? What about the option of full-time Christian work—how do I know if that's my calling?

CORE AREA 1
EVANGELISM/IMPACT ON CAMPUS

CORE AREA 2
ACADEMICS/GETTING THE GRADES

CORE AREA 3
ENGAGEMENT/USING YOUR MIND

CORE AREA 4
FOLLOW-THROUGH/YOUR NEXT LIFE STAGE

The final chapter is a call to action. Being a student isn't just for a few years in one's late teens and twenties. It's for *all* followers of Christ, forever. Whether or not we're enrolling for a graduate degree, we have to still follow through. Because if we're Christ's disciples, then we are students for life!

For many, the college years are great years, perhaps even the best years of our lives. Let's make the most of them.

12. CRUCIAL COUNSEL FOR CAMPUS MINISTERS:
Healthy Campus Ministry

I know the power of campus ministry. I've been personally involved in the baptisms of hundreds (especially campus-aged) and witnessed thousands more going down into the waters of baptism. Like many of you, I was reached through campus ministry. During my first forty-eight hours at college two committed Christians approached me and invited me to take Christ more seriously. The men whose lives I admired most in those early days of my faith were campus ministers. They lit a fire in our hearts. Their impact was exponential: students affecting their fellow students, communities, and nations—out of proportion to their numbers.

Five years later I would head up our nascent University of London outreach. We had some challenging times in London, and we had some great times, too. Our most memorable term was probably autumn 1988. When the term began, there were sixty students in the ministry. By the time we broke for the Christmas holidays, we were over 100! Most of those forty-four young disciples went on to do great things for the Lord.

All told, I served ten years as a campus minister at over twenty universities.[92] You too have been serving in campus ministry. You've experienced how rewarding it can be. Several things that make campus ministry work especially attractive are the *openness* of the students, the *simplicity* of their life situations (fewer distractions), their *youth* (vibrancy) and, once again, their *impact* as future leaders in their various fields. Campus ministry is an amazing harvest field (Matt 9:37). You know how essential it is to raise up leaders, given the magnitude of the task. Otherwise you may burn out, taking on too many responsibilities.

Please allow a personal note. Many of you have invited me to speak in your campus ministry (workshops, debates, leaders' meetings, class series). Thank you! I've been truly inspired to meet so many new disciples—the fruit of your labor. I genuinely admire what you have accomplished in your "harvest field." Wherever I travel—Anchorage, Atlanta, Boston, Brasilia, Chicago, Cincinnati, Denver, Hampton Roads, Los Angeles, Riga, San Antonio, Singapore—and meet the new campus Christians, I am thrilled. In fact, I find it difficult to begin my sermons without bragging about campus work around the world (Prov 25:25). At the same time, I'm quite sure I have unfairly omitted many other great campus works—some may be smaller ministries, or I may have simply forgotten. Of course I have heard about many great works going on outside my own church tradition, yet I share most often about the ministries with which I am most familiar (my own circle).

At any rate, given our common understanding of the importance of your work, please accept me as a colleague, speaking to you respectfully but frankly (Prov 15:22; 20:18; 24:26) about what it takes to foster a healthy campus ministry atmosphere. I'll share a dozen baseline convictions about healthy campus ministries, followed by a dozen practical points of action.

1. Academics

First, students need to flourish academically. While it is true that God in his providence has put them on the college campus to win others to the cause of Christ, they are also there to study. God is not honored by substandard work, and we can help campus disciples do well academically by carefully designing the campus ministry schedule.

God asks that we complete our work with all of our heart "as working for the Lord," which means students need to study as if studying for Christ himself (Col 3:23). This means the campus ministry must be streamlined, not clogged with meetings and complicated programs that interfere with study time or disrupt healthy study rhythms. Today's students often have to work part-time jobs as well, which means that a lack of strategic planning on the campus minister's part can make it difficult for both the campus student and the ministry to succeed.

2. Family

Second, students need good communication with their families. In an era when so many family relationships are already distant or strained, we do students a disservice when we fail to encourage them to work to strengthen or maintain their relationships with siblings and parents, who in many cases have often sacrificed in order for them to attend college. Christian students are grateful students.

Prepare students for interactions with family during holiday breaks and vacations from school. If you have done a good job nurturing them in the faith—no matter how young spiritually they are—they should do fine. Even outside the more structured atmosphere of the campus ministry, help the student develop strong convictions to walk with the Lord through daily meditation on the word, prayer, and seeking his will. Before the student leaves for break, make sure to take time to set up a plan for communication, especially if the student will be absent from the campus ministry for an extended period of time. If the student lives close by, take the time to introduce yourself to the family. It goes a long way to strengthen relationships when parents have a face to go with the name of the campus minister. Your interaction with them will demonstrate that you want the best for their child.

Finally, especially in cases where campus students come from dysfunctional or broken families, don't forget that, though you may be only a few years older, you are serving as a sort of spiritual father or mother. As a spiritual parent to the campus student, do not forget that some students may need help in other areas of their life, not just spiritually. Campus ministry is a wonderful setting for you as a leader to manifest Christ's love in relationships and studies with students (Gal 5:6).

3. Counseling

Campus leaders are de facto counselors, whether or not they are trained therapists. Every person is different, and each situation is different. To meet people's needs, we can't treat everyone the same, as though all students were generic or interchangeable. Yet that *can become* the approach if we give identical advice to everyone; utilize the same study series (with the same verses) for everyone; or if we're too busy to hear everyone's story. We must teach Christ to people (Eph 4:20–21), yet the Bible never gives an exact sequence of topics to be covered, nor does it even tell us how to proclaim Christ (Col 1:28–2:1).

When you could use some input on how best to approach a member or visitor to the ministry, never hesitate to seek out a trusted person like an elder in the church. Young men and women thrive in a climate of wise counsel, nurtured by encouragement and support from their leaders. When they're receiving help in such areas as academics, relationships, and spiritual health, they will also flourish evangelistically. Students love to talk, and strong Christian students will find the urge to talk about Jesus Christ irresistible.

When I was younger, I thought people just *decided* to obey the truth. Conversion was all about saying "yes" to God and "no" to sin. I still believe that, but the reality isn't so one-dimensional. That's why assembly-line mechanical approaches to evangelism are high on converts, low on retention. What affects behavior?

Three factors affect an individual's behavior: brain development and chemistry, family systems, and personal choice. If we don't view people holistically, taking account of all three aspects, our counsel can be ineffective. We may even damage the faith of the person we're trying to help. If you're not familiar with a holistic approach, you will find a fuller explanation in Appendix B.[93]

4. Outreach

In keeping with the advice above, it follows that every person deserves to be treated uniquely with his or her own emotional makeup in mind. Tailor your personal Bible studies to the individual. Set study series (like First Principles or Guard the Gospel) are fine, but remember the following three caveats:

- Understand that there's no evidence of a "study series" in the New Testament. There are *lists* of core teaching (like Ephesians 4:3–6), but the jury is out on how often people met to discuss the gospel. In Acts 17 Paul presented the message to the Jews on three occasions. Were there other meetings, or private discussions with more individualized counseling? Who can say? When we take our cherished approach too seriously, or treat it as sacrosanct, then it becomes difficult to consider alternatives.[94]

- Use the studies that *this* person needs. For example, Guard the Gospel has thirty-five studies for non-Christians. As long as the basics of the gospel are covered, it is a matter of opinion how many sessions are needed.

- Move at the right pace for that person. You know you're going too fast if coercion is the only way to get "progress," and too slow if you notice the person being distracted or filling his schedule with other activities.

5. Other Groups on Campus

Campus leaders, please be respectful towards other groups on campus—especially religious groups. As much as possible, view them as allies, not enemies (Mark 9:38–41; Luke 9:49–50). When we feel threatened, it's easier to react out of anxiety, creating adversarial relationships with those outside our immediate fellowship circle. Things will go much more smoothly without the sense of rivalry. In my case, a more collegial strategy has led to good publicity, newspaper articles, television appearances, and large numbers of visitors—one time over 1000 guests came to a campus event!

Further, this type of inclusive, friendly approach works well in the workplace and beyond the campus ministry. Eventually, when the students enter the workforce, they will likely not be surrounded by hundreds of likeminded people who make decisions to the same spiritual standard they do. Learning how to interact positively with those who think differently, while maintaining biblical convictions, will prove invaluable.

6. Scriptural Knowledge

In 2015 I recorded a podcast, "Why Christian Leaders Need to Be Exceptionally Good Bible Students."[95] The title gives away my conviction! I believe this is also your conviction—or it should be. A few pointers may be helpful:

- Be careful about the proof-texting method. Simply asserting a truth by linking it to a scripture, without teaching how you arrived at your interpretation, is problematic. How do you *know* your group has it right? What about other interpretations? The questions to ask are, "What does the passage mean? What was the Holy Spirit trying to tell the people back then?"

- Leaders should certainly stand out by their grasp of Scripture and in their ability to perform exegesis properly. Have you read the entire Bible? (How many times?) Are you stuck in reading a single translation? Do you consult a few reference works and extrabiblical sources in your studies of Scripture? How do you approach Scripture memorization?

- Share with the ministry what you've been learning in your personal study. For me as a preacher and teacher, my personal studies are by far my best source for insight, conviction, and teaching material. When the students know you are under the authority of Scripture, they will be more confident of your leadership, and your motives.

- More and more ministry training centers are requiring campus ministers to receive at least a basic diploma in biblical studies.[96] This is a healthy trend, and a good *beginning*. May the trend continue.

7. Apologetics

A basic mastery of Christian evidences is an essential part of training for campus ministry in the 21st century. Without it, we may reach the odd atheist (though not many), or an occasional skeptic who has turned his or her back on Christianity, but most of those who doubt or disbelieve will not be reached. Yet I have heard ministers deny the importance of apologetics. "We haven't found it made much difference." But was it done *well?* Were those invited to apologetic events people who had no major questions in the first place? If we're reaching only lapsed evangelicals, who already believed in God and the Bible, the bias will be self-confirming. If we want to reach the entire world—most of whom are Muslims, Hindus, Buddhists, and secular atheists—we cannot do without apologetics.

8. Relating to University Officials

Much has already been said about the importance of working *with* university authorities. Make sure you are not only registered as a club, but are also aware of, and following, the rules permitting operating on campus. If you ever catch wind of a problem, don't ignore it or ask Joe to take care of it. Get involved. (Sorry, Joe.)

9. Welcoming Future Students

Reach out to high school students in your church and help them begin to dream about being part of the campus ministry. Are you occasionally inviting the older high school students to campus events? Do you seek these older teens out in the fellowship at church? Encourage your ministry to be inclusive and set an example of relationship building to the younger students in high school. This will encourage growth of the individuals and your ministry as a whole.

10. Student Jobs

College is expensive. Students will need to work if they are going to graduate in four years (in the US—in many countries it's three years), as opposed to drawing out the process (more and more students need five years, and an enormous percentage never finish at all). Most students today work a part-time job. How many hours a campus student should work, so that they can still study and be fully active in the campus ministry, is a matter of opinion. Here are my thoughts on student work schedules:

- 8–16 hours a week seems to be ideal, allowing sufficient time to excel academically, sleep enough to stay healthy, have daily time for personal devotions, and be well integrated into the campus ministry.

- 16–24 hours seems to be around the maximum students with full course loads can work, in order to get decent grades and be actively involved in campus ministry.

- 24–32 hours might work for exceptionally disciplined students, but the majority will not be able to carry a full load of classes *and* do well academically and spiritually. Fatigue, poor health, skipping classes, inconsistent spiritual commitment—a price is paid for overdoing it. Note: 20–30 hours seems to work fine for half-time students.

• 32–40 hours is considered working full time. At this point, with few exceptions, the student will be enrolled part time in college. The risk of this student never graduating increases.

Let's look out for the students. Encourage them to have the right priorities. Encourage them to spend wisely, give generously, save when possible, and plan for the future. If you're wondering what counsel to give them, imagine that student's father or mother is sitting in the room with you. What would you say?

11. Ministry Meeting Schedule
Closely connected with student jobs, schedule planning on your part should take into account all of the students' needs. That means it should be flexible, changing with the academic year. Three or four meetings a week is ample (Sunday church, a student devotional, evangelistic Bible discussion, and a leaders' meeting for those with the time and talent).

Be in tune with the scheduling of events on campus. For example, if there are a lot of parties (like fraternities and sororities) and people are prone to going out on Fridays, schedule something on Fridays as a fun alternative. Conversely, if the university has an exciting football team, don't be hesitant to be known as that fun-loving group whose sports parties are awesome (even though they're not worldly). Think twice before creating a schedule that eats up every evening or weekends, with little time for recreation or homework.

During exam times, keep meetings to a minimum (one or two a week). It was my custom to allow leaders with semester GPAs under 3.0 to take a break from leaders' meetings so that they could reorder their priorities. When leaders are performing poorly in their classes, a poor model is presented to everybody else, who may conclude, "I guess doing well in college is less important than spiritual stuff." And that's a false antithesis! Every situation will be different, of course, but still leaders *should* be held to a higher standard, academics included.

12. Faith
Students need to grow spiritually. Just as discipline is crucial for

academic life, so too is discipline crucial for spiritual life. Many students want to change the world. They deeply desire to live sacrificially and admire those who embody the high ideals of Christ in their lifestyle. Faith is contagious; it emboldens men and women to do great things, to serve, to lead. My final area of conviction is that we as campus leaders must model what we expect: faith. When we are living on the edge (not on edge and irritable, or on the emotional ragged edge), our plain Christian living is worth a thousand explanations, programs, and meetings.

We have highlighted a number of crucial convictions for the campus leaders to have and share with the students whom they influence. Additional specifics and details follow, so that these ideals aren't ethereal, but concrete. First, as a campus leader, be sure to take a second look at Chapters 2 and 3 before your term, semester, or quarter begins. You can also help the students by giving them edifying gifts; see the suggestions in Appendix C for book ideas. For now, however, a quick checklist may be most helpful.

Checklist for Campus Leaders

- Am I determined to be a man or woman of the Word? Model integrity in your own study of the Word.
- Am I trained in biblical interpretation? Do my lessons have depth? Are my points the ones inherent in my text, or am I forcing my interpretation on the text?
- Am I continually building up my knowledge of apologetics, becoming more capable of engaging with skeptics, and answering questions and assuaging doubts *within* the campus ministry?
- What are my plans this year for my own continuing education?
- If I too am a student, am I striving to lead the way in spiritual and academic excellence?
- Are we converting students to the truth of the gospel or to the doctrinal correctness of our own church group?
- How sensitive is our campus evangelism (see Chapter 3)?
- Is our organization set up legally on campus? Do I know—and am I determined to respect—the official regulations of the university?
- Is the campus meeting schedule reasonable? Do the students'

schedules "breathe?"

- Do I bring in guest speakers from time to time, or does every lesson have to be done by me?
- Am I treating non-Christian students with gentleness and respect? Do I view people holistically?
- Do we have an academic awards program to recognize and emphasize the importance of academic discipline and achievement?
- Do I regularly ask our students how they are doing in the four areas of health, academics, finances, and family relations?
- When students are financially stressed, having to put in so many work hours that it's affecting their grades (and even their health), what am I willing to do to lighten the load?
- Am I supportive of students' decisions regarding graduate education? When they share their plans, do I try to redirect their thinking for the best of *my* ministry, or am I truly thinking of their long-term prospects?
- Do the high school students in the local church *want* to be part of the campus group? If not, what can I change?
- Am I aware of any sensitive medical or psychological conditions within the group? (Program the numbers of counselors and therapists in your phone, so that you may easily make referrals when necessary.)
- Am I too busy to get to know the parents and other family members of those in the campus ministry? Am I assuring parents that I have their sons' and daughters' best interests in mind, not only in the area of academics, but also with regard to their health, career, happiness, and other areas? Am I solicitous of their input? ("What are some ways I could reinforce your priorities in molding the character of your son/daughter?")
- Am I reproducing myself, raising up new campus leaders?
- How many of the students reached in my ministry are still faithful disciples after one year? Five years? Ten years?

Healthy Campus Ministry?
As with any part of the body of Christ, the spiritual health of a campus ministry is much more than rapid numerical growth. In campus

ministry, we're laying a foundation for life—including life skills, growth in character and integrity, and much more—so that sixty or seventy years later the students are still faithful to Christ. If this is not the case, let's have the courage to look in the mirror *and* into the Word and ask why not. (The material in Appendix B may also help us to think through *how* we are building.)

A healthy long-term perspective should keep us from falling into the trap of seeking quick yet unrooted growth (Mark 4:17). Those who make their confession of faith at a relatively young age will go on to do great things for the Lord—the vast majority in their families, careers, and ministries, a handful as full-time Christian workers—holding fast that confession till they have finished running the race (Heb 12:1–2).

---

[92] In London primarily, but also in Sydney, Birmingham, Stockholm, Philadelphia, and Washington DC.

[93] Further, I suggest you look into becoming a member of the American Association of Christian Counselors. Take their basic course; remain a member for about $90 a year. It is not necessary to be a full-time or even part-time counselor to join. Check out www.aacc.net.

[94] In my own fellowship of churches, when another evangelist and I suggested a more flexible approach to working with seekers, there was considerable resistance from many of the older leaders.

[95] http://www.douglasjacoby.com/why-christian-leaders-need-to-be-exceptionally-good-bible-students/.

[96] The program I direct, AIM (and its affiliates) is the equivalent of 1.5 college semesters, taught over the span of two to three years.

13. FULL-TIME CHRISTIAN WORK:
God's Will for Me?

Quite naturally, many college students, and especially those led to Christ as students, aspire to become campus ministers, missionaries, and other full-time Christian workers. They want to be like those whose organization, personal example, and energy have touched so many lives. Although I wouldn't admit it at first, after a year or two in Christ I was enthralled with the idea of becoming a campus minister. And I'm so happy that I ended up having the opportunity to go on staff. Back then, interns had to raise their own support. The church didn't pay any salary until you became an evangelist or women's ministry leader. The training I received (especially from Douglas Arthur, with whom I served through the greater part of twenty-five years), the challenges we met, and the amazing things the Lord enabled us to accomplish—I wouldn't trade for anything.

Yet full-time Christian work is for only a small minority. Not everyone is gifted for such ministry (with the vital skills that complement their type-A wiring), nor is unlimited funding available for hiring. Missions committees and local churches must be discerning. But you too need to be discerning.

There's no doubt that zealous, college-educated, spiritual self-starters often make excellent staff members, in whatever capacity they serve. If you've been considering full-time Christian work, count the cost first. To make a wise and timely decision, ask yourself:

- Do I have what it takes? Church work, including campus ministry, is hard work. (I did it for twenty years, and speak from experience.) How's my work ethic? (Ask others for a more objective answer.)
- What is the record in my first few years in the Lord? How do I do under pressure? Have many people been converted to Christ through me?
- How are my grades? Those who go on staff should have a

proven record of *discipline*. Grades are one indicator.

- Should I take a year off? If I'm unsure, a year off may be a good idea (some sort of internship or "one-year challenge"). However, this might not be responsible if I'm in debt (I should be working and paying off my debt—Rom 13:8), have major family responsibilities, or am falling behind in coursework and will end up needing extra semesters to graduate.

- How would I be a "tentmaker"? In passages like Acts 18 we see that Paul and some of his ministry associates took "secular" jobs as necessary in order not to be a burden on the church. If I were full time in the ministry of the Word, what skill could I fall back on for lean times or in the event I became unemployed? Am I thinking realistically, or do I think that somehow the church will "bail me out" if I end up in financial straits?

- Have I considered graduate education? It's an excellent way to develop your "tentmaker" side. (Please don't skip the next chapter.)

- Have I thought this through? 80% of people who go on staff are dismissed, some after a short time, others after ten or twenty years, or even longer. That statistic should sober me.

- Am I taking the long view? I may be young, but if I don't begin saving now—particularly building up some sort of retirement fund—I could be in trouble in the golden years, and may be a burden on others.

- What's my plan for biblical training? We increase our chances of being hired, and being retained, with a credential: a Bible degree, counseling certification, or professional skill that could enable me to make a lateral move within the scope of church employment.

- Have I received a *written job description*? If my prospective employer is unwilling to provide this, there may be some significant "boundary" issues in that ministry.

- Will I obtain a *written contract*? Most jobs entail a contract, signed by both parties, the employer and the employee. How much of the salary goes into benefits or a retirement account? What are the terms of severance, in case I'm let go? If I'm asked to relocate, who pays the moving costs? Contracts *protect* the staff member.

- If I'm married or may marry, have I thought through what this means for my spouse? Some ministries insist that both spouses work for the church, although others allow the husband to serve alone, or the wife to serve part time (especially when the kids are young, or when there are health, family, or other challenges).

- Am I prepared for pushback from family or friends? Not everyone will appreciate my conviction, and there may be consequences, tension or even termination of relationships.

- Will I become a dropout? If your leaders encourage you to drop out of college, or "finish the degree later," run for the hills. Responsibility before God means owning up to our responsibilities, not procrastinating.[97] Let's not use church as an excuse for taking the path of least resistance.

The Ministry or Not the Ministry?

It is beyond dispute that the Lord needs solid, faithful men and women whose work is the ministry of the Word (Acts 6:4). Might I be one of those who would flourish more and contribute more in such a setting? There is always a need for dedicated full-time workers. This is a matter for counsel (Prov 15:22), prayer (James 1:5), and careful consideration (Luke 14:28).

Whatever you decide, don't get pulled into unbiblical thinking that only staff members are "in the ministry." In a healthy church, the vast majority of ministering is done not by the minority of members (type-A full-time Christian workers), but by the majority (non–staff members with "secular jobs"); see Ephesians 4:16.

Every Christian, regardless of whether he or she is ever supported financially by the body of Christ, is in the ministry. The question is not between ministry and nonministry, but of *what kind* of ministry?

---

[97] Etymological note: *pro* (for) + *crās* (tomorrow) are the roots of Latin *procrastinare,* to put off for tomorrow.

14. THE NEXT STEP:
Grad School?

Many students wonder if graduate school is the next step for them. That depends on the individual. Will a master's degree in your field enable you to command a higher salary? Is this an open time in terms of your schedule, so that you can devote further years to school? Is postgraduate study something you're enthused about? Would you like to increase your annual income by 30% (over $1000/month)? Are you considering grad school simply as a way to stay in the campus ministry? While grad school may not be for everyone, I've seen that the majority of undergraduates will benefit in multiple ways if they invest the extra years to go for the next degree.

Taking a Year Off?

Maybe postgraduate education *is* for you, but just not right now. It may help to take a year off between degrees. Now might be a time for you to work and save the money you'll need for the next degree. Or perhaps money isn't an issue. In that case, this could be a great time to see the world, or devote a year to serving in a ministry overseas or domestically. If you have grown more attractive during your year off—picked up a technical skill, gained work experience, grown in your understanding of the world—your prospective graduate school may view you more positively. On the other hand, maybe you are wired differently, and would prefer to get all your education finished at one go. All these questions are important to consider before making the decision to take a break from academics.

Is a Master's Degree for Me?

There are many benefits to consider:

- You'll enter the workforce as a more mature person, even if by only a couple of years.
- If you enjoy teaching, you will probably need a master's degree first. This is a standard requirement in public schools as well as in universities.

- If you're heading for a doctorate (as a professional or a professor), a master's will almost certainly be your middle step.

- In nearly every field, a master's degree will increase your salary by over 30%, and a doctorate by nearly 50%. Research the expected return on investment for advanced degrees in your field. For instance, if you have no desire to teach, an advanced degree in chemistry might not be worth the student loans you would need to take out to fund it. If your deepest desire is to be a stay-at-home mom, consider whether time and money spent on your master's degree is worth it. However, if you have a marketable degree which increases your salary, you will be able to spend more, save more, and give more away (the simple formula we tried to teach our children). Besides, to reduce financial dependence on others is biblical (1 Thess 4:12).

- The more qualified you are, the higher you are likely to rise in your profession. Therefore, it makes sense to invest in building your skills, and earning an advanced degree will do that.

Do you see a man skillful in his work?
He will stand before kings;
he will not stand before obscure men (Prov 22:29 ESV).[98]

COLLEGE-EDUCATED 25- TO 34-YEAR-OLDS
Latest Available Figures (Pew Research Center[99])

MEDIAN INCOME	MONTHLY	ANNUAL
Professional & Doctorate:	$5415	$64,980 +49%
Master's degree:	$4772	$57,264 +31%
Bachelor's degree:	$3643	$43,716 —
High school graduate:	$2259	$27,108 -38%

Doctorates

There are two kinds of doctorate degrees, professional (like DVM, DPsy, DMin, and JD[100]) and academic (PhD, ThD). Let's consider the pluses and minuses.

- *Teaching* – If you hold a doctorate, you can teach graduate students at a university level.

- *Access* – You can also easily access professional networks, many of which require an advanced degree for membership.

- *Prestige* – Holders of doctorates command a high level of respect in society.

- *Expense* – Doctorates are expensive, especially PhDs.[101]

- *Time* – A doctorate degree takes a long time to earn, easily lengthening your years in university. Academic doctorates normally require four to eight years, while professional doctorates typically take three years. You can easily end up spending over a decade earning three degrees.

In short, doctorates require a heavy investment of cash and time, yet they may open doors that would otherwise remain forever closed. Because they are so hard to earn, and the degree holder is expected to be an expert, doctorate degrees enhance a person's credibility.

A Word to "Mature" Students

You may not be a traditional college senior trying to decide whether to enroll in a master's program—with hundreds of other 21- and 22-year-olds. You may be decades older! I received my DMin in 1999. I was 39 years old—the youngest in our class! My wife completed her MS in 2014. We were what they call "mature" or nontraditional students.

The point is that it's never too late to go back to school. These days, it is increasingly common to find men and women in their thirties, forties, and fifties studying for bachelors, masters, and doctorate degrees. Don't let age hold you back if you feel ready for the next step. The academic challenge might even serve to keep you young; an active mind is well known to confer numerous health advantages.

In addition, online learning is becoming increasingly common. (My wife did her master's degree entirely online.) Yep, the world is a-changin', and it's changing fast. The trick is to keep up with all the changes—because that means we're keeping up with people. Let's use our educational opportunities, just as we use technology, to make an impact on the world as we bring glory to God.

---

[98] The Hebrew indicates "man." Ironically, in many graduate programs women now outnumber men. Globally, there are 100 women enrolled in college for every 93 men. Source: http://yaleglobal.yale.edu/content/women-more-educated-men-still-paid-less-men.

[99] Accessed 17/12/15 at http://www.pewresearch.org/fact-tank/2014/02/28/for-millennials-a-bachelors-degree-continues-to-pay-off-but-a-masters-earns-even-more/ft_14-02-26_collegeearnings/.

As an Associated Press article explains, "The field of study in college does seem to matter. Those who studied science or engineering were most likely to say that their current job is 'very closely' related to their college or graduate field of study, at 60 percent, compared to 43 percent for both liberal arts and business majors." Source: http://www.huffingtonpost.com/2014/02/11/earnings-gap-college-grads-high-school_n_4768780.html.

[100] Technically a JD (Juris Doctor, or doctor of law) is a doctorate, though the equivalent is a first degree in the UK and a second degree in the US.

[101] See http://chronicle.com/article/The-Cost-of-a-PhD-Students/144049/.

15. AFTER COLLEGE:
Students for Life

You've reached the end of the book (though, hopefully, not the end of the line). You will be more confident on campus—because Christians should *own* education! You will improve in evangelism, sensitivity, and smart study habits, as well as become a better thinker, able to better represent Christ in the classes you are taking—and for years afterwards.

Maybe you will soon head to grad school, or even train for a position as a missionary or campus minister. You'll appreciate the "crucial counsel" for campus leaders. Throughout, I've tried hard to speak as a friend—not just a lecturer, but also someone who's been through the system and knows what it's like.

Is School Ever Out?
In this final chapter I'd like to leave you with one thought. Out in the world people go to school for twelve years, maybe a couple of years of college—and then (sadly) they stop learning. Which is to say, they stop growing mentally. They power down and pull the plug out of the wall, with no intention of improving themselves mentally or of continuing their education, in any way, shape, or form.

Maybe they've internalized the lyrics of the Alice Cooper song *School's Out*. It was a hit in 1972, when I was in eighth grade. I didn't think much of the message, but the tune sure was catchy. The refrain runs *School's out for summer/School's out forever/School's been blown to pieces,* and the final refrain, *School's out for summer/School's out with fever/School's out completely.* I don't know about Alice, but I don't want people to say of me, "That guy stopped learning a long time ago." And yet—in a culture where *real men* don't read books (though they do flip through magazines)—I sometimes do hear people laugh jokingly, "Aw, I ain't read a book since college (or high school)." Are those words to be uttered with pride, or with shame? Isn't it a tacit admission of apathy, of a mind already made up?

Well, Paul says it's not our job to judge the world. God will take care of that (1 Cor 5:12–13). So let's not get worked up about Alice, or people who've stopped learning. We are, however, to urge and encourage one another within the body of Christ. I have a word for my brothers and sisters in Christ, and it's pretty simple.

Students Who Don't Study?

Disciples who aren't learning, growing, and studying, are a contradiction in terms. You may have heard that the New Testament Greek word *mathētēs*[102] means student, disciple, or pupil. So if you're a disciple, you're a student. Of course knowledge can puff up (1 Cor 8:1), but not knowledge we praise God for and which we share with others in a spirit of love. Education isn't a phase of life for young people, or something you pass through in order to mature. We're to have the attitude of a student *at all times, and for all our lives.* We're to have the heart and humility of a child. So, does the old dog learn new tricks?

Depth and Breadth

Apart from Jesus, whose intelligence was indisputably off the charts,[103] and Paul, the best educated of Jesus' apostles, there is a third biblical figure who inspires me by his mind. He makes me want to be a student *for life.* I admire Solomon not only for his *depth* of knowledge, but also for his *breadth.* Many people are brilliant in their areas of expertise, but move outside that arena and they have little to say—one-trick ponies, so to say. Before he drifted away from the Lord (in his old age), Solomon was a shining example for those who love to learn, who take pleasure in discovering God's world and know that others too are captivated.

> *God gave Solomon wisdom and very great insight, and a breadth of understanding as measureless as the sand on the seashore... He spoke three thousand proverbs and his songs numbered a thousand and five. He spoke about plant life, from the cedar of Lebanon to the hyssop that grows out of walls. He also spoke about animals and birds, reptiles and fish. From all nations people came to listen to Solomon's wisdom, sent by all the kings of the world, who had heard of his wisdom* (1 Kings 4:29, 32–34).

Notice the following:

- His education was *broad*. He seems to have taken pleasure in learning across multiple subjects—a sort of "Renaissance man." Yet in a few areas it was also *deep*.

- While several hundred of Solomon's proverbs are in the book by that name, thousands more have been lost to posterity. Like the Bible itself, only a small fraction of divine wisdom comes to us—no more than we need, and a perennial reminder to remain humble.

- He crystalized his learning so that others could benefit (Eccl 12:9–11). There's not much point in studying like Solomon without a method for passing it on to others.

- It wasn't only the humanities that held his interest, but also the natural sciences—and even then he was interested in everything he could see. Solomon was a student of both botany *and* zoology. Just imagine what he would have done if the microscope and the telescope had been invented 2500 years earlier!

- His learning was not merely technical. He composed a prodigious number of songs. He was an architect, landscape designer, and engineer (1 Kings 3:1; Eccl 2:4), but also deeply fond of music (1 Kings 4:32; Eccl 2:8).

- Others not only heard the king's proverbs and songs; some traveled great distances and brought lavish gifts just for a personal audience with him (1 Kings 10:1–13). Glory was given to God even outside the people of Israel, as foreigners were impacted by, and hopefully infected by, Solomon's love of learning about God's world and passion to express truth in words, notes, and books.

Maybe a page or two ago you were bracing yourself for a challenge: to study the Scriptures, improve your GPA, or reread your college textbooks after graduation (not that I've ever done that). Instead, the challenge is to continue learning in two directions—out and down, for breadth and for depth. What does this mean, then, for the disciple who gets the point—that we should never stop learning, and that the day we do, we have begun to die? Because if we're not learning, we've forgotten the initial call to come and be Christ's disciples, his students.

If nothing else, we should at least be enthusiastic about learning how to have the mind of Christ (1 Cor 2:16). While the central book for a Christian has to be the Bible, on which we are charged to meditate daily (Josh 1:8; Ps 1:2; 119:9–16; Col 3:16), there are *thousands* of helpful works to enable us to go deeper in our study of the Word. Appendix C (by contrast) may seem a meager offering, but do take a look, as some of the suggestions may be just right for where you are spiritually at this point in your life.

Yet learning doesn't have to be centered solely on religious subjects. Why not keep learning about other things in the world, too (like Solomon)? It helps keep me humble when my study reminds me of how little hard science I know, or how many languages I cannot speak, or how few great works of literature I'm familiar with, or how useless I would be in the operating room — or the garage, for that matter. It also makes me respect others for the expertise they have in their fields of work or study.

To be truly broad, we need to study not just the Word but also the *world*. Yet how are we going to be able to manage that, with the busyness of life and the thousand distractions that come our way? There are two character traits that will make the way easier.

- First, *vigilance*. The Bible repeatedly tells us to keep alert. Peter reminds us, "Be sober-minded; be watchful. Your adversary the devil prowls around like a roaring lion, seeking someone to devour" (1 Pet 5:8 ESV). Since drugs and alcohol dull the mind and reduce vigilance, it follows that we need to be careful that we don't lose our *spiritual* sobriety. If our eyes aren't truly open, no wonder we miss the cues the Lord has thrown our way; no wonder we're so easily distracted by things that really don't matter! Stay awake.

- Second, *self-motivation*. The Lord nudges us to learn from the ant (Prov 6:6–11). Once you leave school, there will probably be no one on your back quizzing you about your reading. But the ant is a self-starter. In Proverbs, the ant is the opposite of the sluggard, one of whose chief traits is oversleeping. He just can't be bothered. Maybe it's obvious that I love to expand my horizons, read a lot, and feel inspired and alive when I'm learning new things. After college I didn't *stop* reading; I began to study *more*. Most of what I know today I learned after university. People often ask me how I find the time. Well, we *make* the time. People make time for whatever they think is important. How important is being a disciple to you?

There you have it. Study the Word. Study the world. Stay alert. Keep motivated. That's how you can remain in the learning mode. No matter what our age, talent, experience, challenges, if we're disciples we're students—for life.

---

[102] There's even a special word in the New Testament for a female disciple, *mathētria*. It appears only once. You can find it in Acts 9:36.

[103] Jesus was highly intelligent—not just as a scholar of the Scriptures (Luke 2:41-47), but as a student of human nature (John 2:25). As you read the gospels, try to see how his mind works when he is in a tight spot (Matthew 21:23-27; 22:15-21). His logical mind is truly brilliant—and yet he never bullies others with his intellect, but rather remains humble in every interaction. Listen to the Jesus podcast at http://www.douglasjacoby.com/jesusmp3/.

APPENDIX A
Paying for My Education

College these days isn't the way it used to be. (More philosophically, as the late Yogi Berra put it, "The future ain't what it used to be.") Financial pressures on students today are unbelievable. When I was a student, few of us *had* to work. The only reason I did was to have some spending money—mainly for the church contribution.[104] At Duke I worked for the Math Department, grading papers and tests. At Harvard, I did janitorial, secretarial, and clerical work. I also had summer work cleaning toilets.

What about now? Tuition levels have quadrupled since my time. Duke tuition was around $5000 a year—now it's $49,000. (Harvard Divinity School was a meager $9000.) The cost of four-year tuition can be like buying a house! I hear more and more stories of graduates carrying $50,000 in debt. (To my readers in other countries, this must sound insane. It is.) I'm meeting men and women who just graduated with masters and doctorates who are $100,000 or even a quarter million in debt! That's not good. What does this mean for students nowadays? How can we be smart about this?

SHOP AROUND

College education is a service available for purchase. The price varies with the market. Not every university charges $50,000 a year. Quite a few studies have come out in recent years ranking institutions not only for their quality of education, but also for their real value in financial terms. Special focus has been placed on how many graduates find jobs, as surveyed across both colleges and courses (engineering grads, psychology students, and so on).[105]

There are five main sources for funding tuition (six, counting grandparents). In order, they are:
- Savings
- Scholarships

- Grants
- Loans
- Work

SOURCES OF FUNDING

Savings
Everyone knows college isn't free. That's actually not true; some are, although you may graduate with certain commitments—like living on an aircraft carrier. (Or maybe something less exciting.) We also know that fees have skyrocketed. There is therefore little excuse for not having planned ahead (Prov 22:3). If savings into a college fund begins at birth—if your parents had foresight—you will have been able to defray a good part of your tuition. When I entered college, I cleaned out my savings, cashed in my bonds, and was able to pay for half of my first semester. Okay, so it didn't go all that far, but it was a start—and I took pride in the fact that I was "all in"—invested in my education.[106]

Scholarships
Thousands of different scholarships are available, some offering $1000 a year, others giving you a "full ride." All three of our children won scholarships. As a result, none left college in debt. But you have to shop around! Talk to your adviser for guidance.

Grants
Colleges are used to applicants counting on significant financial aid. A grant is something the college gives you. It isn't a loan—you don't need to pay it back. Most colleges, and certainly the elite ones, offer this sort of aid to most if not all of their students!

Work
Whether it's a job through the university, or something outside, companies count on the relatively cheap labor of hiring students for part-time work. If you are already working full time, perhaps attending night school, you are in a different position. You probably didn't secure your job through the university. Keep in mind that the number of hours a week to which you commit affects not only time available for assignments, but also your alertness. Allow time for *life*—being with

friends, sleeping, taking a break if you need to.

Loans

Ideally, you won't need to take out any loans to finish your degree. The following equation describes the ideal:

$$Sa + Sc + G + W = F_c$$

Savings + Scholarships + Grant + Work = college Fees, ideally. But if you do have to borrow, take repaying them seriously—otherwise you may be forced to repay through garnished wages or community service. Otherwise your equation will include another variable, L, for loans.

$$Sa + Sc + G + W + L = F_c$$

Some of my friends discourage all debt, and I respect them for their conviction about living within one's means. Yet I would distinguish two types of debt—good debt and bad debt. Nearly every type is bad, since someone is buying something for which he lacks the funds. Consider three types of good debt:

- **Mortgage** for a residence. As long as you keep paying the mortgage, you're fine. Instead of "losing" monthly rent payments, you are purchasing equity in your house or apartment. Taking out a mortgage is generally a good idea, unless you cannot easily make the monthly payments or have a history of overspending. (The stakes are high, since repeated failure to pay will lead to the bank taking possession of the house.)

- **Borrowing from a friend**—for a few days. Sometimes cash flow can be erratic. If you *know* that your paycheck on Friday will allow you to repay the $50 you borrowed from William, and since (presumably) he isn't a loan shark who will charge 50% interest, or break your legs if you don't pay, then that's okay. It's nice that friends help one another out. (My advice to the friend: any time you lend to another person, even if—*and especially if*—that person is a Christian, you should be willing to take a loss. Don't lend out money that you need to pay your own bills. The Proverbs say a lot about this (Prov 6:1–2; 11:15; 17:18; 22:26).

- **College tuition.** Tuition increases your ability to earn, which can make it more of a wise investment than a purchase of something you can't afford. Of course tuition isn't "good" debt if it means twenty years of anxiety as you pay off your student loans, or if no one is hiring trilingual unicyclists, or if fees are higher than other comparable institutions' fees. Still, if you've been wise in the area of savings before college, and are diligent in seeking scholarships and grants, you may avoid having to take out *any* loans—the ideal.

WARNING!

Beware using a credit card to pay tuition! You will end up paying over 25% in interest for the first years, and far, far more after that, as interest compounds. Even putting $5000 on a credit card, if not paid back quickly, you can end up with a debt of $40,000. It's a great deal for the credit card companies—but a horrible one for you.

I was fortunate to graduate from my first university debt-free. Not so with the master's. I was able to arrange two small loans, but they didn't come close to covering the need. Whereas my parents had generously paid two thirds of my undergraduate fees, graduate expenses and fees were up to me. I asked my dad if I could borrow. He said yes, as long as I paid him back in full by his seventieth birthday. I retired that loan a few years early. It was a point of honor. Fees for the third degree—which in my case were only $3000 a year—were covered by my employer.

Let's consider an imaginary scenario for an American student. He or she is applying to a midrange college, neither exorbitant nor cheap (as college goes). You will need to make a similar chart to be able to grasp at a glance your own situation.

COLLEGE FUNDING
A TYPICAL[107] SCENARIO (2 SEMESTERS)

SUPPORT		EXPENSES	
Savings	$8,500	Tuition	$25,000
Scholarships	$4,500	Housing	$7,000
Grant	$11,900	Meals	$5,500
Work	$6,700	Books	$1,100
Loan	$8,800	Other	$1,800
TOTAL	**$40,400**	**TOTAL**	**$40,400**

Assumptions: (1) that you have saved for college through working during high school summers. You may have asked your relatives for cash gifts (to be used for college expenses) during the last few years, and this soon became a considerable sum; (2) you've received two modest scholarships, one for leadership aptitude and another because of your ethnic background; (3) the university has offered a typical grant, which hopefully will cover half of your tuition (though nothing more); (4) you're able to work fifteen hours a week, at a little over minimum wage, as well as during the summer break (full time); and (5) your student loan makes up the difference.

HOW TO LEAVE COLLEGE WITH ZERO DEBT

This may sound nice in theory, but is it realistic to expect adolescent males and females of college age to take responsibility at this level? Isn't it really someone else's job—like the parents'—to figure it out and pay for it all, as many in the current generation seem to believe? Not at all!

It's never too early to learn financial responsibility. How can I guarantee I leave college debt-free? The following pointers are not meant to discourage all loans; some student loans are good, just not if there was a wiser way.

- **Start saving** for college as many years in advance as possible. If you still need more support...

- **Community colleges** are a little-known secret, often offering quality education at a fraction of the cost of the elite university. Attend a community college for two years, and then transfer. Or you may begin at a less expensive college, than transfer into your dream college

- **Go abroad.** Consider a university in another country. Canada, for example, has excellent and (relatively) inexpensive collegiate education.

- **Apply for scholarships.** Don't *not* apply because you find the applications burdensome. Time is money, and if you end up in greater debt, you will have to do some *real* work to pay back your lender with money that could have been yours for free, if only you'd pushed harder in the beginning.

- **Grants.** If your institution offers a grant but it's too low, no one is forcing you to accept it. Write to—or ideally meet with—those making the decisions and see if you can bargain. Or get more scholarship money. Or select a different college.

- **Work hours.** Determine the right working hours for your part-time job. You want to do well academically *and* you want to minimize your indebtedness. That means it's not too bright to work so many hours that your brain is mush. There may be some parts of the semester when you can afford to work more hours, but in "crunch time" you want to be as free as possible to study.

- **Work summers!** True, you may be attracted by other ideas for your "free" time, but unless your summer is funded by someone else and your indebtedness is low, it doesn't make a whole lot of sense to ignore loans (Prov 10:5). It makes even less sense to go even further into debt when you had the summer before you. Begin chipping away at them.

- **Finish early.** For some students, it's a good plan to finish an academic term or two early by taking classes in the summer. If you're in high school, jump at any courses you can take that confer college credit. At an average American college, one course costs $1000–$2000. Do the math.

- **Loan terms.** If you do end up taking out loans, make sure you understand the terms before signing on the dotted line. Of course this would mean you're not graduating debt-free, but you can still reach that point soon after finishing school if you manage your spending and earning.

- **False security.** Reject the false sense of security that says, "My loans aren't due for repayment until sometime after I stop being a student. I have plenty of time—I don't need to begin thinking about this yet." Again, the Bible has many passages urging us to prepare for the future (Prov 24:30–34; Luke 12:19).

- **Balance your accounts**—always. When I failed to do this in grad school, along with an unhealthy habit of using the ATM machine to find out how much I could withdraw, I bounced six checks in a row. $100 in fees—ouch! When you want to know your bank balance, be sure to add the balance showing online or in the ATM *minus* any checks that haven't yet cleared, or upcoming automatic payments. That's the *only* way to know where you really stand!

- **Slow down.** If you're going into greater debt every term, it may make sense to decelerate. Take three or four classes instead of five. It's not a catastrophe if you need an extra semester or two to graduate. This is a way you can lower expenses (tuition) while raising income (salary).

- **Seek counsel.** It is likely that in your family, community, or church there are men and women who know how to handle money responsibly (Prov 12:15; 15:12). Seek them out. (They might even offer you a free meal!)

- **Spend modestly during college years.** Do you enjoy Starbucks coffee? Great. But if your $5 coffee is a daily habit, you can rack up $1000 a year in caffeination expenses. If you are on the meal plan, don't eat out. If your plan was to cook in your own apartment, don't triple costs by restaurants or takeaway. Eating out twice a week, assuming meal and tip come to $10, mounts up to another $1000 per year. The truth is, most students are lax in tracking their expenditures not because they are young and irresponsible, but because they're like everyone else—*most* people find this to be a hassle, and so take the easy way.

Conclusion

If you're someone who takes advice, the suggestions in this appendix will ensure you'll be in a stronger financial position after graduation. It would be nice if we didn't have to work our way through college, or have to make the effort to strategize. Yet the experience you'll gain as you take ownership of your financial life will soften the blow when—hopefully one day soon—you land on your feet in the working world.

Finally, remember that good things are seldom free. When it comes to schooling, we all pay for our education—or lack of it.

---

[104] My offering was about $5 a week during my bachelor's degree, $10–20 during my master's—I suppose the amount now would be doubled or tripled, given inflation. Although it's not the point of this chapter, it's still important for students to give, regardless of the economy. If they can afford to pay $10 for a pizza, they can afford to put $10 into the plate. (I suspect most could give more, if they managed their personal finances with discipline.)

[105] If you live in the US, you may want to check out resources like https://www.collegeboard.org and https://fafsa.ed.gov.

[106] Between savings and scholarship money, I was able to fund one full year's tuition. That meant my parents only had to pay for two years of my undergraduate education.

[107] The College Board reported average tuition and fees (2015–2016 school year) of $32,405 at private colleges, $9,410 as state residents at public colleges, and $23,893 for out-of-state residents. Source: http://www.collegedata.com/cs/content/content_payarticle_tmpl.jhtml?articleId=.

APPENDIX B
Holistic Campus Ministry

As we counsel disciples or evangelize the lost, we're likely to be most successful when our approach takes into account three aspects[108] of the individual: the volitional (will and choice), the relational (connections with others, from family of origin onward), and the neurochemical (what's going on in the brain). Rather than viewing members or prospective members of your campus ministry in a *simplistic* manner ("If I show them what's right, they'll certainly change—unless they have a bad heart"), they need us to approach them *holistically*. Of course we need to get down to the nitty-gritty, asking specific questions, but people are far more than the sum of their vices and virtues. Such a flat perception does a disservice to those we serve.

1. Freewill decisions – Ownership of choices. We *can* say yes to God and no to sin (Titus 2:11–12). We should expect people to be responsible, honest, sincere, and decisive; there *is* something black and white about repentance. Yet some choices aren't made on the spot; they may take months or even years. Even after someone has surrendered to Christ, there may still be residual sins and sinful patterns. Or there may be parts of their lives of which they are so ashamed that they open up only after a period of time in Christ, when they feel safe in doing so. As one example of Christians who make the clean break from sin, take the Ephesians. We read in Acts 19:18–19 that some believers came totally clean about the sin of witchcraft—one on the "Galatians 5 list" (Gal 5:20)—only *after* they were converted. As these believers grew in their appreciation of the awesome power of Christ, their thinking changed at the root level (Acts 19:11–17).

The Spirit changes us. Many negative patterns and habits change only after one has been in Christ for some time. Some more binary thinkers might doubt their conversion: "If they didn't confess this before their baptism, then their conversion was invalid." But there's a different way to look at the situation. They renounced one aspect of their past (sorcery) *because* the Spirit had been working in their lives. Besides, while the Scriptures connect confession with forgiveness (Prov 28:13), they do not direct us to take an exhaustive inventory of the person's life. (Few would be competent for such a task, anyway.) A "sin list," when seekers list their sins on paper, may help *them* see how far they are from God, but unless the same level of specificity is sought in asking questions about their relationships and family of origin, physical and mental health, and possible therapy or medications, then isn't the practice shortsighted, focusing more on choices than on contributing causes to those choices?

2. Family of origin – Effects of relationships. Humans are relational creatures. We aren't individuals so much as members of family systems. Without knowledge of how someone functioned in his or her family of origin, we do not truly know that person. How people perceive reality, respond under stress, and relate to others has a lot to do with how they were brought up. Patterns of behavior and reaction to stressors, for example, are normally modeled on what children see in the household. If certain patterns are to be broken—instead of being carried forward to yet another generation—then the family system must be taken into account. Roles need to be addressed to increase "differentiation" and decrease "fusion." This means taking more time to get to know people. If they ever seem "stuck," probe gently. Behaviors change when patterns change, especially as the Spirit of Christ transforms our lives.

Negative generational patterns *can* be broken, but seldom immediately. Basic concepts of family systems, like emotional differentiation and fusion, triangles, identified patients, and communication styles, truly matter. To study the Bible with someone without knowing how they've been conditioned in their family of origin is to risk missing something truly important. Ask questions. Then we will more easily discern people's "default positions" and the stressors in their lives, so that our counsel will be suited to the individual.[109]

Of course we're shaped by more than our families of origin. We all have multiple relationships that affect us, some weakly, some strongly. Relationships with persons with whom we bond later in life may closely resemble relationships in our family of origin (father-daughter, older brother-younger brother, etc.), as patterns tend to be perpetuated. The point is that we aren't *just* individuals; we all exist in a matrix of relationships, with clearly defined patterns of interaction.

3. Brain chemistry – Influence of hormones.[110] Body chemistry, or physiology, including the influences of powerful neurotransmitters, powerfully affects behavior. We all know that we may behave differently than normal when we're dehydrated or we haven't eaten in a while and our blood sugar has fallen. (In my case, I'm a little less lucid and a lot more impatient.) But the behavioral factor we're focusing on here is neurochemistry. This is the third component of the person you're hoping to win for Christ or counsel in the context of campus ministry. Brain chemistry is complicated. That should come as no surprise, given that the human brain is the most complex object in the entire universe. (That may sound like an exaggeration, but it's true—far more complex than all the galaxies and nebulae.)

Neuroscientists, psychiatrists, and psychologists strive to understand the profound connections between brain chemistry and behavior. Some behaviors are unlikely to be modified without counsel that takes into account the chemistry and development[111] of the brain (serotonin, adrenalin, norepinephrine, and other hormones). Of course advances in neuroscience don't mean sin isn't wrong, or that all wrongdoing is "illness," or that our lives are scripted by the genes we inherited. Nevertheless, a different picture of human thinking and action is emerging. Being current with these discoveries should make us more effective in evangelism, counseling, family, and fellowship.

We need to appreciate the way the brain works, and I am convinced that it is when we bring patient understanding and nonjudgmental acceptance to those we seek to help that the gospel message and the Spirit of Christ have their most transformative effect. Towards this end, ministry leaders need to be familiar with the basics of neuroscience. They also need to know *when* to refer, and to *whom* to make referrals.

A related matter is the role of medications, whether drugs that attack depression or drugs that flatten out the highs and lows of the bipolar cycle. How much do *you* understand about the neurological effects of commonly prescribed drugs?[112] Many times young leaders have assumed that in Christ there is no need for counseling, therapy, or medication.[113] They have persuaded new converts to quit going to counseling or stop taking their pills—often with disastrous effect. Even after a non-Christian has been converted, the neural network remains, and the process of "rewiring" may take years.

Another implication of the neurochemical side of people is that we must know when and where to make a referral.[114] It is illegal to practice psychiatry without a license, or to set yourself up as a psychologist without credentialed training. Credentials aren't necessarily sufficient in order to be a Christian counselor, but some degree of training is necessary. Which counselors in the university counseling center do you know? Do you tacitly discourage members of your campus ministry from taking advantage of such resources?

One last tip: Don't tamper with people's medications. If you think someone needs to come off his or her pills, the patient should be referred to the primary care physician or psychiatrist. (Psychologists and counselors cannot prescribe medications, since they are not physicians.[115]) Only a trained and certified expert should advise decisions related to medication.

We Know Less Than We Think

Reading this appendix, you might be tempted to conclude that trying to help another human being, whether in evangelism or in counseling, is hopelessly complicated. Yet that is not the case. The word of God is still living and active, and obedience to God's word still sets people free. Regardless of our training, we still have a mission: to reach the world as faithful messengers (Heb 4:12; John 8:32; 2 Cor 5:18–20). This requires us to be urgent (not paralyzed in befuddlement), confident in the power of God to change hearts (not demoralized at the thought of needing to read stacks of books on counseling!).

True humility will certainly not lead us to silence. True humility impels us to rely on the Lord for the power, to delve into his word for the truth, to seek advice when we lack wisdom, and to be ready to go where he sends us—to a lost world.

That's what humility does. A humble person isn't taciturn or gloomy, but vocal, joyous with the Spirit, determined to obey the Lord. The right spirit is caught in the words of Carnell:

> Whoever meditates on the mystery of his own life will quickly realize why only God, the searcher of the secrets of the heart, can pass final judgment. We cannot judge what we have no access to. The self is a swirling conflict of fears, impulses, sentiments, interests, allergies, and foibles. It is a metaphysical given for which there is no easy rational explanation. Now if we cannot unveil the mystery of our own motives and affections, how much less can we unveil the mystery in others? That is, as we look into ourselves, we encounter the mystery of our own, the depths of our own selfhood… And having recognized the mysteries that dwell in the very depths of our being, how can we treat other people as if they were empty or superficial beings, without the same kind of mystery?[116]

Conclusion

People are complicated. Understanding that their feelings, behaviors, and relationships are all more complex than we may have realized should make us cautious to judge (Prov 16:2), humbled by the state of our ignorance and awed by God's immeasurable grace. It's not that the Bible doesn't provide the solutions, but we value quick results, and easily misread cues or jump to conclusions. Maybe that's why there's such an emphasis on grace, patience, and forgiveness in the Scriptures.

The Bible embodies a full-orbed understanding of humans and human behavior. This more nuanced view also makes sense of why the Lord justifies some biblical characters despite egregious sins and weakness (David—adultery; Noah—drunkenness; Sarah—meanness; and so on). Scripture clearly indicates that we are responsible for the decisions we make. Yet our degree of responsibility is affected by our perception of reality, which is significantly influenced by deep and systematic patterns of relationships with others as well as by brain chemistry and development. We may think we have an objective picture of who people are, and what their motives are—though Paul certainly didn't make such a bold claim (1 Cor 4:1–5). We all make errors in judgment. We cannot eliminate them, but we can prevent many of them. Fortunately the Lord is the Righteous Judge, who takes all things into account and holds us no more or less accountable than we actually are.

---

[108] Christian counselors will typically embrace a fourfold approach to mental health diagnosis and treatment:

- Psychological (temperament, worldview, etc.)
- Social (family of origin issues, relationship issues)
- Biological (genetics, physical illness, predisposition to certain disorders)
- Spiritual (which is often the only aspect that campus ministers are qualified to deal with)

[109] A standard text on family systems is Edwin H. Friedman's *Generation to Generation: Family Process in Church and Synagogue*. http://www.amazon.com/dp/B00E84JUSM/ref=nosim?tag=dougjaco-20&linkCode=sb1&camp=212353&creative=380549.

[110] Although serotonin, norepinephrine, etc. are, technically, hormones, they're better described as neurotransmitters. Most hormones are free-flowing signaling chemicals that are secreted by glands. Some of them act as neuromodulators (like adrenaline), but hormones are analog (can work to varying degrees) while neurotransmitters are digital (on or off).

[111] It's not just brain chemistry that shapes who we are, but also brain development and organization. Certain disorders, e.g. schizophrenia, have been shown to be linked to actual cytoarchitectonic and structural differences in the brain. Disorders like ADHD and learning disabilities are neurodevelopmental, not neurochemical. Someone with a neurodevelopmental problem (like a learning disorder) may find it difficult to process certain concepts.

[112] See *Rejoice Always: A Handbook for Christians Facing Emotional Challenges,* by Drs. Michael and Mary Shapiro.

[113] Within my own fellowship, back in the 1970s and 1980s we used to recommend Jay Adams' *Competent to Counsel,* a book that denies the reality of mental illness, discourages medication, and is deeply distrustful of mental health professionals. Everything comes down to sin. Adams taught that the solution to our problems is repentance, and counselors need to lovingly challenge those who are struggling.

[114] You may want to explain to someone you refer that it is unethical for a mental

health professional to impose his or her worldview on the client. Therefore, when going into therapy, the Christian must first make it clear to the therapist that they will not do anything contrary to the Bible (e.g., some therapists might tell a Christian who is struggling with same-sex attraction to indulge this impulse for a while to decide if that's his or her true "identity"). In other words, we urge people seeking therapy to be assertive at the outset, and to also thoroughly vet the clinician by asking about credentials, areas of specialty, years of experience, etc. *Caveat emptor.*

[115] I'm generalizing. Psychologists can prescribe in some states in the US, on a limited basis.

[116] Edward John Carnell, inaugural presidential address, Fuller Theological Seminary, 1955.

APPENDIX C
Must-Have Books for Christian Students

NEWLY CONVERTED

Be Still, My Soul: A Practical Guide to a Deeper Relationship with God, by Sam Laing
www.ipibooks.com

Basic Christianity, by John R. W. Stott
www.amazon.com

The Lion Never Sleeps: Preparing Those You Love for Satan's Attacks, by Mike Taliaferro
www.ipibooks.com

A Quick Overview of the Bible: Understanding How All the Pieces Fit Together, by Douglas Jacoby
www.ipibooks.com

Getting the Most from the Bible (Second Edition), by Steve Kinnard
www.ipibooks.com

FOR ALL DISCIPLES

Caring Beyond the Margins: What Every Christian Needs to Know About Homosexuality, by Guy Hammond
www.ipibooks.com

The Disciplined Life: The Mark of Christian Maturity, by Richard S. Taylor
www.amazon.com

How to Read a Book: The Classic Guide to Intelligent Reading, by Mortimer J. Adler and Charles Van Dorn
www.amazon.com

Humility: The Beauty of Holiness, by Andrew Murray
www.amazon.com

The Lion Handbook to the Bible
www.amazon.com

Mere Christianity, by C. S. Lewis
www.amazon.com

The Prideful Soul's Guide to Humility, by Thomas A. Jones and
Michael Fontenot
www.ipibooks.com

Repentance: A Cosmic Shift of Mind and Heart, by Edward J. Anton. To be reprinted by 2017.
www.ipibooks.com

Romans: The Heart Set Free, by Gordon Ferguson
www.ipibooks.com

The Screwtape Letters, by C.S. Lewis
www.amazon.com

Set Apart: Calling a Worldly Church to a Godly Life, by R. Kent
Hughes
www.amazon.com

Shining Like Stars: An Evangelism Handbook, by Douglas Jacoby
www.ipibooks.com

*Spiritual Leadership: A Commitment to Excellence for Every
Believer,* by J. Oswald Sanders
www.amazon.com

Strong in the Grace: Reclaiming the Heart of the Gospel,
by Thomas A. Jones
www.ipibooks.com

Will the Real Heretics Please Stand Up: A New Look at Today's Evangelical Church in the Light of Early Christianity, by David W. Bercot
www.ipibooks.com

Your Bible Questions Answered, by Douglas Jacoby
www.ipibooks.com

FOR MATURE BELIEVERS

Compelling Evidence for God and the Bible: Finding the Truth in an Age of Doubt, by Douglas Jacoby
www.ipibooks.com

The Imitation of Christ, by Thomas à Kempis
www.amazon.com

The Pilgrim's Progress, by John Bunyan
www.amazon.com

A Serious Call to a Devout and Holy Life, by William Law
www.amazon.com

HIGH SCHOOL STUDENTS

Getting Into College, by Rachel Korn and Jennifer Y. Kabat, eds.
www.amazon.com

Making the Most of College: Students Speak Their Minds, by Richard J. Light
www.amazon.com

Preparing for College: Practical Advice for Students and their Families, by John F. Reardon
www.amazon.com

The Six Most Important Decisions You'll Ever Make: A Guide for Teens, by Sean Covey
www.amazon.com

CAMPUS LEADERS

Biblical Preaching: The Development and Delivery of Expository Messages, by Haddon Robinson
www.amazon.com

Boundaries: When to Say Yes, How to Say No to Take Control of your Life, by Henry Cloud and John Townsend
www.amazon.com

The Emotionally Healthy Church: A Strategy for Discipleship That Actually Changes Lives, by Peter Scazzero
www.amazon.com

Dynamic Leadership: Principles, Roles and Relationships for a Life-Changing Church, by Gordon Ferguson
www.ipibooks.com

Friend or Foe? (video), by Douglas Jacoby
www.ipibooks.com

Golden Rule Leadership: Building a Spirit of Team and Family in the Body of Christ, by Gordon Ferguson and Wyndham Shaw
www.ipibooks.com

How to Read the Bible for All Its Worth, by Gordon Fee and Douglas Stuart
www.amazon.com

Prepared to Answer: Restoring Truth in an Age of Relativism, by Gordon Ferguson
www.ipibooks.com

Rejoice Always: A Handbook for Christians Facing Emotional Challenges, by Drs. Michael and Mary Shapiro (to be reprinted in 2017).
www.ipibooks.com

The Spirit: The Work of the Holy Spirit in the Lives of Disciples, by Douglas Jacoby
www.ipibooks.com

Tactics: A Game Plan for Discussing Your Christian Convictions, by Greg Koukl
www.amazon.com

Who Is My Brother: Facing a Crisis of Identity & Fellowship, by F. LaGard Smith
www.amazon.com

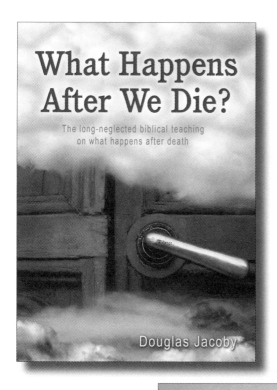

Available at
www.ipibooks.com

Available at
www.ipibooks.com

An Evangelism Handbook
Fifth Edition

Shining
Like
STARS

Douglas Jacoby

Available at
www.ipibooks.com

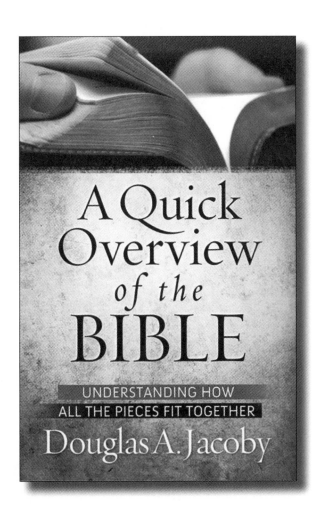

Available at
www.ipibooks.com

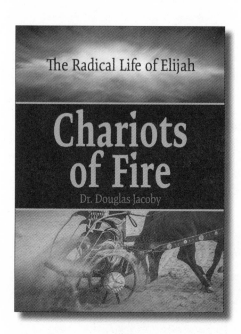

Available at
www.ipibooks.com

Available at
www.ipibooks.com

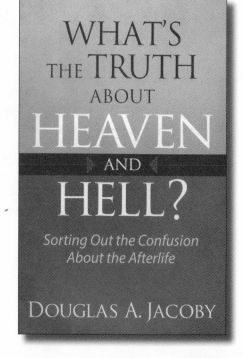

www.DouglasJacoby.com

- Over 10,000 pages of Christian resource material.

- Become a website member for even more—articles, Bible studies, biblical character studies, and other podcasts.

- Sign up for weekly updates, each with a practical Bible study.

www.ipibooks.com